POMPEY

LEADERSHIP ▪ STRATEGY ▪ CONFLICT

NIC FIELDS ▪ ILLUSTRATED BY PETER DENNIS

First published in 2012 by Osprey Publishing
Midland House, West Way, Botley, Oxford OX2 0PH, UK
44-02 23rd St, Suite 219, Long Island City, NY 11101, USA

E-mail: info@ospreypublishing.com

Print ISBN: 978 1 84908 572 4
PDF e-book ISBN: 978 1 84908 573 1
EPUB e-book ISBN: 978 1 78096 045 6

Editorial by Ilios Publishing Ltd, Oxford, UK (www.iliospublishing.com)
Cartography: Mapping Specialists Ltd.
Design by Myriam Bell Design, UK
Index by Marie-Pierre Evans
Originated by PDQ Digital Media Solutions, Suffolk, UK
Printed in China through Worldprint Ltd

12 13 14 15 16   10 9 8 7 6 5 4 3 2 1

A CIP catalogue record for this book is available from the British Library.

www.ospreypublishing.com

Artist's note

Readers may care to note that the original paintings from which the
colour plates in this book were prepared are available for private sale.
All reproduction copyright whatsoever is retained by the Publishers.
All enquiries should be addressed to:

Peter Dennis, Fieldhead, The Park, Mansfield, NG18 2AT, United
Kingdom
magie.h@ntlworld.com

The Publishers regret that they can enter into no correspondence upon
this matter.

Front-cover image credit

Topfoto

The Woodland Trust

Osprey Publishing are supporting the Woodland Trust, the UK's leading
woodland conservation charity, by funding the dedication of trees.

Abbreviations

App. *BC*	Appian *Bellum civilia*
App. *Mith.*	Appian *Mithridatica*
Burstein	S. M. Burstein, *Translated Documents of Greece and Rome 3: The Hellenistic Age from the battle of Ipsos to the death of Kleopatra VII* (Cambridge, 1985)
Caes. *BC*	Caesar *Bellum civile*
Caes. *BG*	Caesar *Bellum Gallicum*
Cic. *Att.*	Cicero *Epistulae ad Atticum*
Cic. *fam.*	Cicero *Epistulae ad familiares*
Cic. *off.*	Cicero *de officiis*
Cic. *Phil.*	Cicero *Philippics*
Cic. *rep.*	Cicero *de re publica*
Dio	Cassius Dio
Flor.	Florus *Epitome*
Front. *Strat.*	Frontinus *Strategemata*
ILS	H. Dessau, *Inscriptiones Latinae Selectae* (Berlin, 1962)
ILLRP	A. Degrassi, *Inscriptiones Latinae Liberae Rei Publicae* (Firenze, 1963–65)
Luc.	Lucan *Pharsalia*
Plin. *HN*	Pliny *Historia Naturalis*
Plut. *Caes.*	Plutarch *Caesar*
Plut. *Lucull.*	Plutarch *Lucullus*
Plut. *Pomp.*	Plutarch *Pompey*
Plut. *Sert.*	Plutarch *Sertorius*
Sall. *Hist.*	Sallust *Historiae*
Suet. *DI*	Suetonius *Divus Iulius*
Val. Max.	Valerius Maximus
Vell.	Velleius Paterculus *Historiae Romanae*

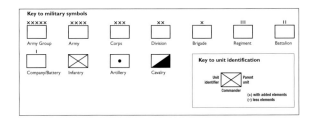

CONTENTS

INTRODUCTION

Cnaeus Pompeius Magnus was a complex character, and in many ways an enigma. Better known to the English-speaking world as Pompey the Great, his persona, like every other man's, had two sides, though in him it stretched to extremes. There was something of Jekyll and Hyde in Pompey. One side, the bright side, shows him as a great man who was brilliant, patriotic and talented. The other, the dark side, shows him as a wilful monster: cruel, arrogant and overbearing. It may be added that his successes tended to go to his head. Both views of Pompey are equally true. He was also a genius, an occasional worker of military miracles, and a man of action. Pompey needed adulation. Everything about him was bigger, starker and more calculating than life. He was not a cool-headed man. Like a Homeric prince in his arrogant and insolent grace he would weep and rage and preen, boasting of his tremendous exploits and anticipating with horror the possibility of his decline. He figures so prominently in the events of the late Republic that he comes across as a giant of a fellow, a figure of colossal stature towering over his opponents, many of whom no doubt saw him (not being of patrician birth) as a braggart and a boor.

Those are the barest of facts. We all know what Caesar made of them, and history, truth and fair play took a frightful beating. Two powerful weapons may be employed against an enemy: the pen and the sword. Caesar was master of both. The sword is supported by courage and skill, and these he had aplenty. The pen conquers either by verity or by fabrication, and here he could easily act the part of Ulysses by relating false facts or by misrepresenting true ones. There is magic in words when they are handled skilfully, and Caesar was a born patrician and a writer of genius.

I am not suggesting that Caesar's *commentarii* contain more of the invention than matter of fact, far from it, but one puts them down feeling that the great Pompey deserves something better. Splendid as they are in print, they are misleading. Whilst they rightly emphasize that Pompey wanted to be the constitutional servant of the state that depended helplessly on his military muscle, they wrongly imply, perhaps for reasons of ideology or of jealousy plain and simple, that he was a coward and a nincompoop.

Whatever he lacked it was not physical courage. One feels obligated to ask why. After all, he was a man, the Roman Alexander, who triumphed in a flood of success and of blood at the age of 24, and became, by way of his second triumph, consul without ever holding any previous elected magistracy at the age of 35. To a man second only to the Macedonian Alexander in his military accomplishments, and some said not even second, to a man who strutted across the stage of the late Republic as if he was a god, breathing mystery and power, came the shadow of the artful reporter. Here we are strongly reminded of Talleyrand's one-line aphorism, if a lie gets only an hour's start it will never be overtaken. Thus history was rewritten, the rebel became legitimate, and the loser is the rebel. Had Pompey been fortunate, instead of suffering defeat and death, he also might have taken up the pen. After all, a genius for self-promotion was to be one of the defining characteristics of Pompey's rapid and remarkable rise to power and glory.

Pompey left no *commentarii* to provide a clear signpost to the inner forces that energized him, to the life lived in his brain. Partisanship, at best, disguises truth. But were we to be unprejudiced, Caesar was an accomplished rogue, and Pompey not one jot better, and equally both felt that the world was too small for the other. Which one of them had the greatest right to rule Rome is no part of the argument; neither of them had any. These two showmen were both consummate performance artists, vying for leadership of Rome's disaffected and downtrodden majority and each attempting to claim Rome's antique grandeur for themselves. Neither were populists, in the literal sense of the term, though they talked a lot about 'the people'. They were both autocrats, admired by the masses, resented by the aristocracy.

Yet Caesar was the autocrat with an acute understanding of the paramount importance of propaganda and presentation in gaining and keeping the political ascendancy, and though unsentimental, he knew the importance attached to symbols in Rome too. Pompey, on the other hand, was neither an astute politician nor an artful propagandist, and he was to destroy himself.

Popularity can be created, and if there was one thing that Caesar could do well, it was propaganda. Popular belief is constant throughout history: in bad times, a single person will emerge to make all the difference and turn everything around. It is familiar today as a drama of the triumph of good over evil, of virtue over vice, of light over darkness. Yet as values change, so does one's evaluation of the past and one's impression of long gone actors. New myths replace the old, and yesterday's villains become today's heroes and vice versa. Heroes are dynamic, seductive people – they would not be heroes otherwise – but what makes heroes in the eyes of the unheroic majority? Usually the conquering of some older, already established strong man, villain or hero.

Marble bust of Pompey (Paris, musée du Louvre, inv. Ma 999), dated to around 70 BC. At the time he was already wildly popular with the Roman masses, and the most celebrated commander of the day. As a young outsider he had won a string of spectacular victories for the Sullan regime in Italy, Sicily and Africa, and more recently in Iberia, for which he was to earn his second triumph and his first consulship. This portrait represents the up-and-coming Pompey: proud, pompous and pretentious, the idol of the people. (Fields-Carré Collection)

Of heroes there are a limited supply, and the hero of our story is one of those fascinating figures upon whom a period of history pivots, but whom history has subsequently ignored. In his own right, he crops up now and then in academic tomes, while at other times his appearances seem shockingly brief only to return to shimmering in the background. This present monograph intends not to describe Pompey exclusively from the viewpoint of the victorious Caesar, hardly the man to do justice to Pompey, but to offer the reader an unbiased treatment of the detail of Pompey's campaigns and estimate him as a commander. Therein lies the purpose of this work, namely to develop the great Pompey as the principal character, not as the second fiddle to the more wordy Caesar.

THE EARLY YEARS

Pompey was born on 29 September 106 BC. His father was Cnaeus Pompeius Strabo, and it was he who gave Pompey his early military training (Vell. 2.29.3, 53.4, Plin. *HN* 37.13). Pompey experienced his first taste of action when he served in his father's army during the Social War (91–88 BC), when his presence at the siege of Asculum in Picenum is guaranteed by the record of Pompeius Strabo's *consilium* (advisory council, *ILLRP* 515.8). He was also present during the ensuing Marian–Octavian tumult (Dio 36.25.2). And so Pompey came of age at a pivotal and worrisome moment in Rome's history, a time that was marked by the marching and countermarching of armies, by political confusion, by muddled loyalties and by harsh reckonings meted out to the losers.

Pompey was to inherit not only the largest private estate in Italy but also some of his father's unpopularity. On his father's death he was accused, unsuccessfully as it turned out, of helping himself to the spoils of Asculum. His father had held the consulship of 89 BC and in that capacity had fought fiercely against Italian rebels in the north during the Social War, notably taking Asculum by siege and selling any surviving insurgents into slavery. A massacre of Roman citizens at Asculum had heralded the revolt, and it

Panorama of Ascoli Piceno, Marche. Ascoli Piceno is the Asculum in ancient Picenum, and was the first Italian city to rise up against Rome in 91 BC. It was during the siege of the rebel city that the teenage Pompey earned his spurs, serving as one of his father's *contubernales*, or staff officers. After shattering the rebellion in Picenum, Pompeius Strabo would use his influence and army to play a double game in the civil war between Marius and Sulla. (Fototeca ENIT)

was news from Asculum that enabled the Romans to celebrate their first decisive victory of the war. The victorious general had the legal right to the spoils of his victory, and though he was expected to deliver a substantial portion to the public treasury and distribute appropriate rewards to his officers and men, what was left might make him, quite legitimately, a wealthy man. It seems that booty and cash allegedly due to the treasury from the sack of the rebel town had somehow found its way into Pompeius Strabo's own possession, and so might now be recovered from his heir.

A thoroughly dubious and ruthless outsider, Pompeius Strabo comes across as the man whom one admits to society because it is impossible to do otherwise, but who is the friend of nobody. Such was his massive unpopularity that his funeral procession was mobbed and his corpse was ditched in the mud.

His son, Pompey, may have learnt to read by studying a eulogy of his father's achievements, but he was to learn other lessons from the pitiless and perfidious Pompeius Strabo. These included the importance of dissimulation, the unprincipled use of loyal soldiers as a private army, the need to be timely and steadfast in betrayal, the need to establish a web of friendship at Rome (which his father had lacked), the importance of money and the need for discretion in its acquisition, and perhaps above all the importance of public opinion. All these were the lessons that the young Pompey learnt and never forgot.

Pompey remained in Italy during the Cinnan regime, but discreetly retired from the camp of Cinna to the ancestral lands in Picenum after threats were made against his life. He did this so discreetly that it was soon widely rumoured that Cinna had had him murdered. According to Plutarch (*Pomp.* 5.1), it was this suspicion that gave rise to the mutiny that ended in Cinna's death. True or not, for the moment Pompey was content to sit tight and await developments. When warring parties are tearing each other to pieces, an opportunist may step in and take his share. As Sulla and his legions landed unopposed at Brundisium sometime in the spring of 83 BC, it was this elementary law that provided the rationale for what was to follow. Pompey, who was not slow in seeing that a vast number of aristocrats were flocking to Sulla's standard in the hope of reviving their political careers, raised on his own initiative a private army of three whole legions from his father's veterans and *clientalae* in Picenum (Plut. *Pomp.* 6.4, Livy *periochae* 85; cf. App. *BC* 1.80, who says one legion).

To many citizens, soldiering appeared to offer easy money, since Pompey's recruiters likely made promises of good wages and a fat bonus upon discharge.

Panorama of the countryside of Marche. The Marche region is ancient Picenum, the land of those Pompeian warlords, father and son, Pompeius Strabo and Pompeius Magnus. In the quest to position himself as the supreme arbiter of Rome's destiny, the bulk of Pompey's partisans in the senatorial and equestrian orders derived, as was fitting, from the family fiefdom. Afranius, Labienus, Gabinius, amongst others, they were military men of no great distinction, the hungry sons of a poor and populous region on the Adriatic slopes of the Apennines. (Fototeca ENIT)

Iuppiter's blessing: Pompey's first triumph

Pompey had raised a private army, an army with no legal basis, for Sulla's interests and for his own. He then held illegal commands in Sicily and in Africa against Marian remnants. For this grisly affair he was to add the word 'Magnus' to his name and, though not even a senator, to be granted the supreme honour of a triumph, the ultimate accolade for a general deemed to have won a significant victory over a worthy, foreign foe.

The triumph was a procession from the *campus Martius* to the temple of Iuppiter Capitolinus (aka Iuppiter Best and Greatest) on the Capitoline Hill, today's Campidoglio, the most sacred spot in Rome. Here the triumphator gave thanks for his victory, which must have been substantial to merit this sort of celebration. Gaining a triumph was by no means easy; a number of conditions had to be met before the Senate would grant one, and funds had to be voted towards defraying the (astronomical) cost involved. Only elected magistrates with *imperium* (viz. dictator, consul, praetor) could celebrate a triumph and the victory should occur during their period of office. The victory should account for at least 5,000 enemy dead, and the war had to be legitimate in that internal conflicts did not count. Territory needed to be added; regaining lost areas was not sufficient. Peace had to prevail after the conquest and the withdrawal of troops. The triumphator also needed the permission from the Senate to retain his military rank inside the sacred boundaries of Rome, the *pomoerium*, and, uniquely, he was allowed to march through the city with his soldiers in full battle gear (e.g. Polybios 6.15, Livy 3.63, 26.21, 28.38, 31.20, 48, 34.10, 45.35, Val. Max. 2.8.1, 2).

On the big day, a solemn procession, headed by the Senate and including the most glamorous prisoners as well as the booty taken, entered Rome. Behind this, leading his laurel-adorned army, came the triumphator himself. He rode the favourite mode of conveyance for Iuppiter, a gilded circular chariot drawn by a team of four white horses and festooned with laurel branches, a bell, a whip and a phallus. He wore gilded red boots, a flowered tunic and a toga with gold stars on a solid purple ground, and held a laurel branch in his right hand and an ivory sceptre topped with an eagle in his left (e.g. Polybios 6.53, Val. Max. 4.4.5, Plin. *HN* 23.36, 28.7, Zonaras 7.21). The triumphator then ascended the Capitoline Hill and left his laurel branch in Iuppiter's lap, thus signifying that he had no intentions of becoming king of Rome (Plin. *HN* 15.40). In that moment, the king of the gods and semi-divine triumphator became one. His name was then entered in honour into the public records. Quite simply, for the Roman citizen, there was nothing to equal a triumph. When he rode in the triumphal chariot, he knew that he was the best and greatest.

In this reconstruction we see the young Pompey (1) enjoying the roseate glow of anticipated immortality. He is riding high above the streets of Rome in the triumphal chariot (2) and wearing the traditional garb of a triumphator. He is preceded by the captives (3) and spoils taken in war, attended by senators, magistrates and officials (4), and followed by his rowdy, devil-may-care veterans (5), the men who marched and bled for him in Sicily and Africa. For them their general's glorious day was one big orgiastic jamboree. For Pompey, however, the splendour and glory of such a day has just come home to him.

Marble portrait of Sulla (Munich, Glyptothek, inv. 309), probably an Augustan copy of a 2nd-century original. A character of cold, calculating cruelty, this bloodstained dictator ruthlessly crushed all those whom he believed stood in his way. Pompey, however, was disturbingly different. The arrogant upstart told Sulla to his patrician face that more people were concerned with the rising than the setting sun. (Bibi Saint-Pol)

The prospect of plunder was an added attraction, alongside the desire to escape unpleasant personal circumstances. If life was rotten in the tenements of Rome, the countryside of Picenum was not always green and pleasant for its occupants. As with most professional armies, the enlisted men of Pompey's army came from among the poorest. Squalor, disease, ignorance and unemployment encouraged many citizens to seek food and shelter in the military. There were, of course, many experienced soldiers to draw upon, including his father's veterans. They provided the cadres needed to stiffen the inexperienced, many of who were raw and ill-disciplined. Now bent on a policy of adventure, Pompey marched south with his private army to join Sulla, on the first stage of a journey that would lead him to princely power in Rome.

Hailing the young Pompey as *imperator* (App. *BC* 1.80), the appellation traditionally awarded to a victorious general, Sulla ordered the tyro general north to clear Gallia Cisalpina of the Marians. After Sulla's close-run victory outside the walls of Rome, his surviving opponents fled overseas, so Pompey was then ordered to Sicily with six legions and a senatorial grant of extraordinary *imperium pro praetore*. Once there he quickly cleared and secured the island, executing (amongst others) the Marian leader, who was still legally a consul and a benefactor of Pompey, after a show trial. This earned him a reputation for cruelty and the equally insulting appellation of *adulescentulus carnifex*, or 'boy butcher' (Val. Max. 6.2.8). But these were not normal times. The irrational circumstances of a civil war made it impossible to lay down what was or what was not legal, and this war was a moral struggle in which most Romans had lost close friends or relatives in appalling circumstances. No quarter would be offered to the vanquished, *pour encourager les autres* presumably. Besides, Roman politics had become sharpened to exclude compromise, and this political extremism had fallen into violence, illegality and intolerance before 82 BC.

Sicilian killings done with, the fierce young Sullan commander then crossed over to Africa and swiftly defeated the leftover Marians, who had gained the support of a Numidian pretender. Pompey restored the throne to the legitimate King Hiempsal, and was hailed by his victorious troops as *imperator* (Plut. *Pomp.* 12.3). This was the kind of adventurous campaigning in which Pompey, by nature a *condottiere*, revelled. Hot blooded and extraordinarily popular with his men, he in no way resembled the senatorial commanders so typical of the republican establishment. Pompey soon received instructions from Sulla ordering him to discharge all his troops except for one legion, which was to remain in Africa. His men, no doubt having been discreetly encouraged by their chief, had other ideas.

Returning to his native city with a large army flushed with its success and owing loyalty only to him, Pompey hankered after a triumph, but he was met with Sulla's stern opposition. Sulla pointed out that triumphs were for appointed praetors or consuls – a mere boy, not yet 25 years of age, Pompey had yet to hold a quaestorship – and, besides, triumphs for victories over Roman citizens were in bad taste. Pompey fumed, and, unabashed, he insisted, saying ominously that 'more people worshipped the rising than the setting sun' (Plut. *Pomp.* 14.3). Sulla could obviously have crushed Pompey with ease if it came to a real showdown, but he probably felt that this was a quarrel that would bring him more pain than profit. And so, with a peeved cry of 'Let him have his triumph!', the ageing dictator yielded. In addition, and perhaps with a touch of sarcasm, he confirmed the cognomen of 'Magnus' ('the Great'), which had been awarded to Pompey by his army. The title stuck.

Although he was still a young man who was not yet even a member of the Senate, Pompey had quite a high opinion of himself, especially when it came to generalship, and, up to now, he had influenced those with power to gain his ends, rather than holding power himself. Obviously, success in the Sullan revolution had given him self-confidence and dreams of grandeur. A youth of staggering arrogance, already touched by greatness, Pompey's guiding light was ambition. This is a laudable passion when guided by reason, but being possessed in the extreme, and under no control, it proved destructive to many, and in the end to himself.

THE MILITARY LIFE

An important part of the story of Rome is the long series of bitter wars by which it subdued the peoples of Italy, culminating in the fierce and bloody war with the Italian allies known as the Social War, occurring from 91–88 BC. At the same time, the political struggle in Rome was about to acquire an increasingly ferocious character. In 88 BC Lucius Cornelius Sulla became the first Roman commander to march on Rome with his army and to capture the city by force. This extraordinary act was prompted by his desire to maintain his consular command for the First Mithridatic War (89–85 BC).

When he returned to Italy from that war, Sulla marched on his mother city a second time and established control of the state by having himself made a dictator – a hint of many troubles that were to follow. In this capacity, he pushed through a package of reactionary constitutional reforms, what are conveniently called the Sullan constitution. Of importance to our story, however, was the fact that on both occasions he had used a client army of *proletarii*, dependent on their commander for their fortunes and their future, to invade the city and destroy his enemies. After this *ne plus ultra* of political violence, no Roman politico could ever again be certain that his opponents would respect the traditional and unwritten restraints necessary for government by consensus. Civil war was now a distinct possibility.

Lepidan tumult

In 78 BC, with Sulla recently dead, one of his erstwhile lieutenants, the consul Marcus Aemilius Lepidus, attempted to undo the Sullan reforms. However, political opposition from the oligarchy of Sulla caused him to resort to armed revolt, exploiting the tension between Sullan colonists and the indigenous inhabitants in Etruria. In an effort to strengthen his power base he championed the cause of the dispossessed, promising to give back to them the land that Sulla had confiscated for the settlement of his own veteran soldiers. Lepidus sought help from the governor of Gallia Cisalpina too. Meanwhile, what of Pompey? After having supported Lepidus to the consulate and, so it was said, encouraged his seditious plans, Pompey was to turn upon his comrade and save the Sullan regime. It clearly paid to be active in one's own interests during unsettled times.

The following year Lepidus tried to emulate Sulla's march on Rome after the Senate had tried to summon him back from his large, unlawful provincial command. He had not only drawn Gallia Transalpina as his proconsular province but had combined this with part of Gallia Cisalpina the other side of the Alps, a precedent on which Caesar's career would later thrive so dangerously. But Lepidus' troops were to prove less effective, and the Lepidan counter-revolution was to flare and burn 'like a fire in straw' (Orosius 5.22.18). The Senate hurriedly passed a *senatus consultum ultimum*, virtually a declaration of martial law, and assembled Sulla's veterans, asking the able and competent Quintus Lutatius Catulus (*cos.* 78 BC) to save the state. Pompey was granted extraordinary *imperium pro praetore* by the Senate and was instructed to assist Catulus.

While the proconsul held Rome, Pompey advanced north to Gallia Cisalpina, where he vanquished Lepidus' confederate Marcus Iunius Brutus, whose son would achieve lasting fame (or notoriety) as one of Caesar's assassins. Brutus surrendered to Pompey on the condition that his life would be spared. The 'boy butcher' then had him executed. Pompey then struck south, came up with Lepidus at the port town of Cosa in Etruria, and defeated him. However, as Pompey failed to pursue him, Lepidus, with some 21,000 troops, managed to escape to Sardinia. Soon afterwards he fell ill and died, and his battered army, now commanded by an old adversary of Pompey's, the Marian Marcus Perperna, sailed on to Iberia, where they would eventually join Sertorius.

The Via Aemilia, which linked Ariminum to Placentia, heading east through today's Modena. It was here, in what was then the old Roman colony of Mutina in Gallia Cisalpina, that Pompey surrounded Brutus' army (some three legions). Whether Brutus betrayed his army or his army changed sides and betrayed him, it is not known. Anyway, with Pompeian dispatch, Pompey had Brutus executed. (Fields-Carré Collection)

Sertorian lesson

Military commands brought glory, which in turn brought popularity. They also brought tribute money, ransoms and loot, which could be used to purchase power. More obviously, they ensured the command of armies, which the Senate did not have. After the departure of Lepidus for Sardinia, Pompey once again pulled the stunt of refusing to disband his army; he got another extraordinary command. We now pick up the story in Iberia. Two of Pompey's legates, albeit leading small detachments, had already been defeated in their turn when the young general advanced with confidence to engage Sertorius, who was preoccupied with the siege of Lauron, a town possibly somewhere near Saguntum (Sagunto).

A race for control of high ground dominating the town of Lauron was won by Sertorius, but then Pompey closed in behind him, apparently trapping his opponent between his own legions and the town. His confidence is said to have been so great that he sent messengers to the townsfolk inviting them to climb onto their walls and watch as he smashed the enemy. It was only then that he discovered that Sertorius had left 6,000 men in his old camp on high ground, which was now behind Pompey's position. If he deployed his army for a full-scale attack on Sertorius' main force then he would himself be taken in the rear. Apparently, Sertorius, when he learned that Pompey had announced to the citizens of Lauron that deliverance was at hand, 'gave a good laugh and said that to Sulla's pupil … he himself would give a lesson; namely, that a general must look behind him rather than in front of him' (Plut. *Sert.* 18.4). So it turned out. Pompey was forced to sit still and watch impotently as Sertorius prosecuted the siege, for he felt that to withdraw altogether would be an open admission of the superiority of his enemy.

During the siege there were only a couple of areas from which Pompey could secure supplies. One was only a short distance from his camp, but this

Col de Montgenèvre (1,854m), Hautes-Alpes, with the obelisk honouring Napoleon. Having learnt that Perperna was holding the Ligurian pass into Gaul, Pompey was forced to use this watershed pass when making his way to Iberia in 77 BC (Sall. *Hist.* 2.98). He probably skirmished with a few local Gauls en route, but he met no serious opposition, reaching the southernmost bend of the Durance river by mid-September. (Francofranco56)

was continually being raided by Sertorius' local troops, swift of foot and lightly armed after the Iberian fashion; they were accustomed to the wild charge or the ambuscade, and ideally suited in equipment and character for hit-and-run warfare. After a while, Pompey decided that his foraging parties should switch their attention to the more distant area, which Sertorius had deliberately left unmolested. The time required to travel to the area, gather supplies and return ensured that any expedition in this direction could not complete its task in a single day. Yet at first this did not appear to be a serious risk, as there continued to be no sign of enemy activity in this area. Finally, when Pompey's men had become complacent, Sertorius ordered Octavius Graecinus, 'with ten cohorts armed after the Roman fashion, and ten cohorts of lightly armed Iberians along with Tarquitius Priscus and 2,000 horsemen' (Front. *Strat.* 2.5.31) to lay an ambush in a nearby forest.

To avoid detection the ambush was set at night. The following morning, around the third hour, the unsuspecting Pompeian convoy began to lumber into view loaded down with forage and firewood. The sudden violence of the assault by the lightly armed Iberian troops threw the whole convoy into confusion. Before resistance could be organized to this initial assault, the cohorts armed as legionaries emerged from the forest and charged. The Pompeians were cut to pieces, harried in their rout by Priscus and his horsemen.

News of the forest ambush prompted Pompey to despatch a legion under Decimus Laelius to the convoy's rescue, or so he hoped. Priscus' cavalry pretended to give way before this new force, and then slipped round the legion to assault its rear while those who followed up the routers attacked it from the front. As the situation went from bad to worse, Pompey, now desperate to avert total disaster, rapidly got his entire army on the move in the hope of rescuing the rescuers. Sertorius deployed his army in battle order on the opposite hillside, thus forcing Pompey to look on as the ambush mopped up both the convoy and most of Laelius' command.

Pompey experienced a soldier's worst nightmare. He had to watch his troops being killed not much more than a couple of hundred metres away without being able to do a thing about it. It must have been a horrifying and sickening sight. Pompey and others in his army had experienced the excitement of a successful outcome on other fields. By the afternoon, however, his army numbered one-third less than it had at sunrise. His legate, Laelius, had been cut down, and his baggage train had been lost. Frontinus, our only detailed source for this ambush,

Remains of the Via Domitia at the *oppidum* of Ambrussum. This was the first Roman road laid in Gaul, linking Italy to Iberia through Gallia Transalpina, crossing the Alps by one of the easiest passes, the Col de Montgenèvre. Construction was started in 118 BC by the proconsul Cnaeus Domitius Ahenobarbus (*cos.* 124 BC), whose name it thus bore. This was the road Pompey and his army took for Iberia. (Benoît Strépenne)

refs to a lost (and unidentifiable) passage of Livy, which claimed that Pompey suffered some 10,000 casualties during this engagement.

Once the unhappy inhabitants of Lauron realized that their ally was unable to aid them, they surrendered to Sertorius. He permitted the townsfolk to go free, but razed the town itself to the ground in an effort to complete Pompey's humiliation. It was an extremely disappointing end to Pompey's first campaign in the peninsula, a bitter blow to the ego of the 'boy-general' who was likened by his flatterers to Alexander the Great.

Long after Pompey died, the Prussian military theorist Karl von Clausewitz wrote his book entitled *Vom Kriege* (*On War*), in which he presented his ideas concerning the principles of war. The basis of war, he stated, is combat, and a battle avoided is one that a commander knows he will lose. Since 'superiority in numbers becomes every day more decisive' as an engagement draws near, the essence of strategy, to borrow the words of Napoleon, 'is the art of making use of time and space' in such a way that a commander can go into combat with all available forces concentrated against the enemy. Long before either Napoleon or Clausewitz were born, Pompey was acquiring a knowledge of those same principles in the hardest possible way. Outside Lauron time and space had worked against him, and so had the opposition's superiority in skill and numbers.

Sertorius and the Example of the Horses (Basel, Kunstmuseum), a pen–and–ink sketch by Hans Holbein the Younger. Mao Tse-tung defines the essence of guerrilla tactics as follows: 'When guerrillas engage a stronger enemy, they withdraw when he advances; harass him when he stops; strike him when he is weary; pursue him when he withdraws' (*On Guerrilla Warfare* 46). Sertorius did exactly this. In Iberia he remained always the brilliant commando: intense, restless, ruthless and inspired.

THE HOUR OF DESTINY

For Pompey, the Sertorian war had been a hard experience, but it had tempered his abilities. Indeed, his greatest days lay just ahead. After Pompey's return from the military quicksand of Iberia, the Senate and the oligarchy were never free from his manipulations and his somewhat menacing shadow until Caesar made war *cum duce Sullana* at Pharsalus (Luc. 7.307).

Pompey was a loyal servant of the Sullan regime, but at the head of an army he was a servant with terrifying powers. After running Lepidus out of Italy, he had received several orders from the Senate to dismiss his army, yet

A view of the Cathedral (completed 1577) and city walls of Segovie (ancient Segovia), as seen from the Alcázar. The city is the possible site of the battle in 75 BC where Metellus encountered and destroyed Sertorius' trusted quaestor Lucius Hirtuleius and his newly recruited army (Orosius 5.23.12). With Hirtuleius out of the way, Metellus was free to join forces with Pompey, who was operating in the eastern part of the peninsula. (José-Manuel Benito)

he had refused to do so, on one pretext or another, in hopes of being given the command against Sertorius. Likewise, when he returned from Iberia he had turned once again to his brutal wooing of the Senate and insisted on being allowed to stand for consul – the highest office in the state – despite the fact that he was too young and had held no previous elected office, and he backed up his demands by brining his legions menacingly close to Rome.

Sulla had drastically curtailed the powers of the tribunes and enhanced those of the Senate. As consul in 70 BC, Pompey would reverse the balance. In subsequent years he was to see to it that a fair number of tribunes were his supporters and he worked through them, as Caesar was to do later, to bypass the increasingly unhappy Sullan oligarchy and appeal directly to the electorate for consent to the expansion of his privileges and power. Pompey did not play the political game with great tact, but what of his generalship?

The way of the general

Let us first consider strategy. This may be defined as a manoeuvring before battle in order that your opponent may be found in a disadvantage when battle is joined. As Clausewitz saw it, strategy is the use of combat or force, or the threat of combat or force, for the realization or achievement of the military objectives or political purpose of the war. Strategy is thus a means to an end. Naturally the ultimate aim of every commander is to defeat his opponent in the field, but his ability to attain that aim depends at least as much on the movements that precede battle as on tactical efficiency when battle is joined. In other words, manoeuvre is essential in so far as it helps towards the attainment of the 'great strategic objective' – the delivery of a final shattering blow at the enemy.

Actual skill in strategy consists in seeing through the intricacies of the whole situation, and bringing into proper combination forces and influences, though seemingly unrelated, so as to apply the principles of war, and then with boldness of decision and execution appearing with the utmost force before the enemy at some decisive point. 'The principles of war, not merely one principle', writes Liddell Hart, 'can be condensed into a single word – *concentration*... The concentration of strength against weakness.' To be able to concentrate, he continues, one must be able to disperse the opponent's strength, which can only be brought about by the dispersion of one's own strength. 'Your dispersion, his dispersion, your concentration – such is the sequence, and each is a sequel' (1991: 334). And although a sound military plan may not be always so readily conceived, yet any plan that offers decisive results, if it agrees with the principles of war, is as plain and intelligible as these principles themselves, and no more to be rejected than they. There still remains, of course, the hazard of accident in execution, and the apprehension of the enemy's movements upsetting your own; but hazard may also favour as well as disfavour, and will not un-befriend the enterprising any more than the timid.

Now we should consider tactics. 'Tactics teaches the use of armed forces in the engagement; strategy, the use of engagements for the object of the war' (Clausewitz *Vom Kriege* 2.1). Tactics, or close-range manoeuvre and use of troops and their weapons, is at the heart of the military art, the arena where a man must think on his feet. In battle a commander has to ask himself two questions. First, how am I to dispose the different parts of my army? Second, in what sequence shall I bring those different parts into the fight? When the army is composed of simple elements, the solution of these problems is correspondingly easy. The Roman armies of our period of study consisted of a mass of heavily equipped shock troops trained for hand-to-hand fighting, supported by a small auxiliary force of more mobile troops armed for the most part with missile weapons. Thus the customary tactical method was to place the shock troops (viz. legionaries) in the centre and their mobile auxiliaries (viz. cavalry) on the wings.

Much depended on the timing of the action of each part of the army, the art of combining the action of these elements when in contact with the opposition as interdependent

City walls of Pamplona and the Baluarte del Fra Martín de Redín, which date from the late 16th to 18th centuries. In the winter of 75–74 BC Pompey founded the Roman colony of Pompaelo, which became Pamplona, to encourage the unruly locals into a more settled and law-abiding existence. (Miguillen)

parts of a single military organism. It was the custom of the Romans, who fully realized the danger of risking the fortune of the day in one combined and simultaneous effort, to withhold a good portion of the army from the fight. In battle, physical endurance is of the utmost importance and all soldiers in close contact with danger become emotionally if not physically exhausted as the battle proceeds. When writing of ancient warfare, Ardant du Picq notes the great value of the Roman system was that it kept only those units that were necessary at the point of combat and the rest 'outside the immediate sphere of moral tension' (1946: 53). The legion, organized into three separate battle lines, was able to hold one-half to two-thirds of its men outside the danger zone – the zone of demoralisation – in which the remaining half or third was engaged. Ideally, therefore, the first-line cohorts fought the main enemy line to a standstill, but if they were rebuffed or lost momentum or the ranks thinned, the second-line cohorts advanced into the combat zone and the process was repeated. The skill of any Roman

Eastern hyperbole and Pompey's own desire to rival Alexander the Great inspired suspicion of his claims to be a great founder of cities – no less than 39 according to Plutarch (*Pomp*. 45.2). Here we see the surviving ruins of Soloi (only these Corinthian columns of a colonnaded street are left), refounded and renamed Pompeiopolis by Pompey after he had subdued the Cilician pirates and settled them here. (Klaus-Peter Simon)

commander lay in committing his reserve cohorts, fresh troops who were both physically and morally fit, at the right time.

Pompey's military greatness belonged to what modern military theorists call the strategic level of war, for it lay in his clear discernment of the problem and in the admirable rapidity and boldness of the measures that he took to solve it. His two greatest commands, the maritime and the Mithridatic, will serve to best illustrate this point.

Pirate kings

When strong kingdoms with powerful navies existed, piracy was usually reduced to a minimum. Yet the last hundred years of the Republic saw one of the most remarkable developments of piracy that the Mediterranean has ever known, when from mere freebooters the pirates organized themselves into a pirate state with headquarters in Cilicia and Crete. It was the more remarkable that this occurred during a time when the sea was controlled by a single power, which, when it put forth its strength under a capable commander, had no difficulty in putting an end to such malignancy in such a short space of time. The ease with which Pompey finally achieved its suppression has naturally led to a severe condemnation of Rome's

Legionaries on the Altar of Domitius Ahenobarbus (Paris, musée du Louvre, inv. Ma 975). The battering power of the Roman army was provided by the legionary wielding *pilum* and *gladius*. (Fields-Carré Collection)

negligence and apathy in permitting piracy to flourish for so long a period. This is especially so when the alliance formed between Mithridates and the pirates of Cilicia had given the Pontic king command of the Aegean, which in the First Mithridatic War had been nearly fatal to Sulla.

This was partly due to the turmoil of the times, which hindered effective policing of the seas, and partly due to the influence of Roman slave dealers who tolerated the pirates as wholesale purveyors of slaves. The more that the economy was glutted with slaves, the more dependent on them it became. The pirates were the most consistent suppliers. Appian writes that the pirates operated 'in squadrons under pirate chiefs, who were like generals of an army' (*Mith.* §92). At this level of organization they were capable of raiding roads and besieging towns along the coasts of Italy. They even staged predatory raids into the western Mediterranean, where they were reputed to be in contact with various insurgent movements, including Sertorius in Iberia and Spartacus in Italy. 'The pirate is not bound by the rules of war, but is the common enemy of everyone', Cicero thundered to his audience. 'There can be no trusting him, no attempt to bind with mutually agreed treaties' (*off.* 3.107). But most damaging of all, they were intercepting the Roman grain fleets plying between Sicily, Sardinia and Africa and the ports of Italy. As this raised the price of grain and led to shortages in Rome, it became a political question – for the common people of Rome, the *proletarii*, the price of grain was perhaps the most important issue in politics.

At any stage of economic development, navies have always been expensive to build and have required handling by specialized crews. Their construction and operation therefore demanded considerable disposable wealth. However, with the

Marble portrait of Marcus Licinius Crassus (Paris, musée du Louvre). It had been Crassus who had bloodily crushed the rebellion of Spartacus, but it had been Pompey who had stolen most of the credit. Crassus was therefore willing to bankroll some of his stupendous wealth in furthering the career of a potential rival to Pompey. (cjh1452000)

A neoclassical marble statue of Spartacus (Paris, musée du Louvre, inv. CC 259), by Denis Foyatier (1793–1863). En route from Iberia to Italy, Pompey mopped up a band of Spartacan fugitives in the north. With a typical lack of tact and scruple, he used this trifling accomplishment to diminish the credit due to Crassus and claim for himself the glory of ending the slave rebellion of Spartacus. There was from this point on no love lost between Pompey and Crassus. (Fields-Carré Collection)

decline of cereal production in Italy over the last 100 years or so, Rome came to rely heavily on supplies from overseas. Part of the problem was that the maintenance of a navy merely for police duties seemed not to be worth the financial outlay, especially so when anti-pirate operations tended to be lengthy affairs and their success not always guaranteed. In 78 BC the Senate had sent Publius Servilius Vatia (*cos.* 79 BC) against the pirates in southern Anatolia (Lycia, Pamphylia, Isauria); after three years' hard fighting in and out of the rocky inlets there and the mountain fastnesses that stretched beyond them, he earned for himself the cognomen 'Isauricus'. Four years later Marcus Antonius (father of Mark Antony), a praetor, was given wide-ranging powers and considerable resources to fight the pirates. In 72 BC Antonius was defeated by the pirates on Crete, and the fetters with which he had loaded his ships were used by the victorious Cretans to bind Roman captives, 'and so he paid the penalty for his folly' (Flor. 3.7.2). The following year Antonius was compelled to conclude a humiliating peace, which the Senate later rejected. He died in office the same year and was awarded, posthumously and it seems derisively, the cognomen 'Creticus', which would normally signify a victorious campaign, for his pains.

In 68 BC the scourge of piracy struck at the very heart of the Republic itself. At Ostia, where the Tiber met the sea, a pirate fleet sailed into the harbour and burned the consular war fleet as it rode at anchor; the port of Rome went up in flames. By the following year the shortage of grain had become so acute that the *lex Gabinia*, the tribunician bill of Aulus Gabinius, was promulgated and passed. Its tenets granted Pompey, over the heads of existing proconsuls, *imperium pro consulare* and massive military resources with which to combat the pirates. What is more, his command was not for the customary six months but for three years, and encompassed the whole of the Mediterranean and the Black Sea and the entire coastline for a distance of 80km inland (Vell. 2.31.2). The pessimism with which the Roman people regarded even their favourite general's prospects may have been reflected in the length of his commission, but the immediate result was nevertheless a fall in the price of grain.

Under his energetic command, and in a wide-ranging whirlwind campaign, Pompey cleared the western Mediterranean of pirates in 40 days and the eastern Mediterranean and Cilicia in around 50 days or so, and in doing so he added enormously to his prestige. His plan had been an able one. He first closed the Pillars of Hercules, the Hellespont, and the Bosporus, and then divided the Mediterranean into 13 zones – six in the west and seven in the east – to each of which was assigned a fleet under an admiral appointed from Pompey's pool of trusted legates. All areas were swept simultaneously,

Doric metope decorated with a bas relief of a Roman warship (Rome, Museo della Civiltà Romana) with a boarding party of marines on the deck. Despite recent efforts to downplay Pompey's campaign against the pirates, there can be no denying that it revealed his skill in the deployment and use of such naval resources. (Fields-Carré Collection)

in order to prevent the pirates from concentrating, and the impetus was from west to east. Pompey himself was not tied to a particular zone, but kept a fleet of 60 warships at his immediate disposal.

By the end of this remarkable campaign, Pompey's forces had captured 71 ships in combat and a further 306 through surrender. Around 90 of these were classed as warships and fitted with rams. Pompey's treatment of his 20,000 captives showed a shrewd understanding of the causes of piracy, for he knew they would swiftly resume their profession if allowed to return to their coastal communities. The old pirate strongholds were slighted or destroyed and the ex-corsairs and their families were successfully settled in more fertile regions throughout the eastern Mediterranean lands (App. *Mith.* §115). Many went to the coastal city of Soloi in Cilicia, which was revived and renamed Pompeiopolis, and it soon became a prosperous trading community. Raiding and piracy were not permanently eradicated from the Mediterranean, but they would never again reach such epidemic proportions as they did in the early decades of the 1st century BC.

Obverse of silver *denarius* of Sextus Pompeius (London, British Museum, inv. 483.2.1), struck in Sicily around 44–43 BC, which he then controlled, to pay his seamen. It bears the legend 'NEPTVNI'. (Ancient Art & Architecture)

Luckless Lucullus

When Gabinius had proposed his bill, all the senators bar one opposed it. The dissenter was Caesar, who as a young man had been kidnapped by pirates and ransomed for 50 talents (Plut. *Pomp.* 25.4). Two tribunes, Lucius Roscius and Lucius Trebellus, were even willing to act on behalf of the Senate and attempted to intervene, but to no avail. The slick Gabinius used the tactic first employed by Tiberius Gracchus and got the tribes to vote the two pro-senatorial tribunes out of office. They unceremoniously backed down. In 67 BC it seems that Pompey lacked support in the Sullan Senate. During the 70s BC the senators had willingly handed him extraordinary commands, but now he was relying on popular support through the tribunes.

The contrast is remarkable, and the shift came with Pompey's consulship of 70 BC when he restored the tribunician powers, thereby weakening the general supremacy of the Senate, which had been strengthened by Sulla. For its part, the Senate thought that the consulship had solved the problem of what to do with Pompey by allowing him to take his place within the establishment. But crisis followed crisis and consul after consul failed. In the end, Pompey was the only man who could deal with these external threats and thus, as in his pre-establishment days as the extralegal enforcer of Sulla's regime, the maritime command was followed by the Mithridatic one. The redoubtable Pontic king, whom Sulla had humbled but not destroyed, was on the rampage again in Asia. He had been provoked by Rome's acquisition of the nearby kingdom of Bithynia, which had convinced the king that only the defeat of Rome could prevent the steady erosion of his power.

In 74 BC, aware that the Romans had their hands full with Sertorius in Iberia, Mithridates had invaded Bithynia and moved into neighbouring Asia (Third Mithridatic War, 73–63 BC). Fortunately for Catulus and his political

Neptune's favourite: Pompey versus the pirates

Piracy was endemic in the Mediterranean – a long inland sea of islands large and small, with jagged coastlines full of hidden harbours – whenever there was no central sea power strong enough to suppress it. The pirates waylaid and ransacked trading vessels that passed up and down the Mediterranean and swooped down upon poorly protected coastal towns and settlements. From the pillaging of famous shrines in Greece and Asia Minor, they had progressed to raids on Italy itself. For such raids they used small open boats that could go close inshore, rowing into the shallows to avoid any pursuit, and dodging into creeks and darting up rivers. They were fast, ferocious and cocksure.

The seas became so hazardous – even the grain supply of Rome was now in peril – that in 67 BC Pompey was given overriding command to deal with this pirate scourge, and put at his disposal 500 warships, 120,000 infantry, 5,000 cavalry, 24 legates and two quaestors. But the bare figures give an inaccurate idea of Pompey's power and position. As Plutarch plainly put it, Pompey was 'not an admiral, but a monarch' (*Pomp.* 25.1). Popular confidence in Pompey was so great that on the very day of his appointment the price of grain (hence bread) suddenly dropped. For the first time in a very long time authorized fighting ships proceeded to clean everyone and everything out of every watery nook and cranny that had been convenient pirate havens. Pompey swept the Mediterranean free from pirates in a little under three months.

In this scene we are off the headland of Coracesium in Cilicia. The proconsul Pompey is leading the marines of his flagship, a splendid six, in a boarding action against a grappled pirate vessel. Among the officers by his side is that unshakable Pompeian Titus Atius Labienus, a military man from Picenum who owed his career thus far to his service in Pompey's wars. The marines are clambering over the side of their ship, shouting and wielding swords and daggers. The pirates have abandoned their oars and about to launch an armed assault on their war-seasoned assailants.

Funerary monument of the *praefectus* Tiberius Flavius Miccalus (Istanbul, Arkeoloji Müzesi, inv. 73.7 T), dated from the 1st century BC, from Perinthus (Kamara Dere). On the right we see a Roman officer. His *gladius* hangs on the left, the opposite side to that of a legionary, and he probably represents a centurion. For both Pompey and Caesar, tough and dependable centurions were the key to an army's success in battle. (Fields-Carré Collection)

cronies, one of their own was serving as consul that year. Lucius Licinius Lucullus, the man who as quaestor in 88 BC had been the only officer to follow Sulla on his first march on Rome, was sent against the Pontic king with five legions. He was particularly devoted to the dictator's memory and, unlike Pompey, could be trusted to stay true to his dead commander and comrade.

The next four years were to witness a string of victories for Lucullus over Mithridates. In his first independent command Lucullus turned out to be a strategist and tactician of truly exceptional talent who, in spite of limited resources, consistently outmanoeuvred Mithridates and defeated his army either in battle or, by 'making its belly the theatre of war' (Plut. *Lucull.* 11.1), through starvation. By the end of 70 BC the power of Mithridates had been shattered and the king himself was a fugitive, driven across the mountains into neighbouring Armenia, the kingdom of his son-in-law Tigranes II.

Yet despite his enormous success, Lucullus found himself sucked farther and farther east, and with an increasingly demoralized army. Perhaps without the support of the Senate, he crossed the headwaters of the Euphrates and invaded Armenia. The kingdom was on a high plateau with steep mountain ranges, which had been, until quite recently, a patchwork of petty states owing allegiance to different rulers. However, under Tigranes, the self-styled 'king of kings', Armenia began to acquire most of the surrounding territory, building a new capital for himself, the self-named fortress city of Tigranocerta. His jerry-built empire did not survive its first major test, however, for outside Tigranocerta Lucullus defeated Tigranes and continued his pursuit of Mithridates.

In the past, eastern armies had very successfully relied on overwhelming numbers to defeat an enemy, more often than not through a prolonged archery battle. When he saw the Romans approaching, Tigranes famously joked that they were 'too many for ambassadors, and too few for soldiers' (Plut. *Lucull.* 27.4). Lucullus led an army of no more than 16,000 infantry with 3,000 cavalry, mainly Galatian and Thracian auxiliaries, and the Armenian king was extremely sorry that he had only one Roman general to fight. The royal quip provoked much sycophantic mirth. Soon afterwards, Lucullus' legions cut Tigranes' great host to pieces in a matter of hours. Tigranes' showpiece capital was then stormed and literally taken apart. With their customary brutal efficiency, the Romans stripped the city bare, Lucullus taking the royal treasury, and his men everything else.

In 68 BC Mithridates slipped out of Armenia and managed to return to Pontus. In the meantime, Lucullus continued his campaign in the highland kingdom, much to the dismay of his exhausted troops and the Senate. One of the Sullan laws, the *lex de maiestate,* forbade a governor to lead troops beyond the borders of his own province without the express permission of the Senate. What is more, Lucullus was surrounded by soldiers who had been with him for nigh-on six years, men who had marched over mountains and across deserts, zigzagging backwards and forwards chasing an elusive enemy. That winter, there were whispers of how all of Pompey's veterans, merely for fighting rebels and slaves, were already settled down with wives and children and in possession of fertile land. Their own general, on the other hand, was starving his veterans of loot. Little surprise then that a mutiny and smear campaign, orchestrated by Publius Clodius Pulcher, was instigated in order to undo Lucullus. In spite of his skills as a general, the aloof Lucullus lacked the knack of winning his soldiers' affection, and he was deeply unpopular within his army. Clodius, who happened to be Lucullus' brother-in-law and had joined his army hoping for promotion and profit, saw an opportunity to present himself as 'the soldier's friend' (Plut. *Lucull.* 34.3) and succeeded in stirring up their passions.

Lucullus was also hated by many influential groups back in Rome, in particular the equestrian businessmen, or *publicani,* whose tax-farming companies operated in the provinces. Lucullus, a humane and highly cultivated man possessing a genuine concern for the well-being of the empire's subjects, had severely curtailed the illegal activities of many of their agents, a measure that did much to win back the loyalty of the provincials to Rome. Back home, however, the general had become the target of violent criticism by various tribunes in the pay of the business lobby. On the point of total victory, Lucullus was thus starved of troops and resources, while his command was gradually dismantled around him (Plut. *Lucull.* 20.5, App. *Mith.* §83).

The following year, while Pompey was enjoying his success at sea, the irrepressible Mithridates popped up with yet another army and won a series of quick victories over the Roman occupying forces. Near Zela (Zilleh, Turkey), for instance, a certain legate by the name of Triarius was trounced by Mithridates, his army apparently losing no less than 24 military tribunes and 150 centurions. Lucullus could only watch in impotent fury as Mithridates and Tigranes recovered most of their home kingdoms. It must have seemed to him that his fierce campaigns had not brought about pacification.

As his world collapsed around him, Lucullus was given a rare moment of satisfaction when he heard the news that his pestiferous brother-in-law had been captured by Cilician pirates. Having absconded from Lucullus' camp after stirring up the mutiny, Clodius had headed west and paid a visit to another of his brothers-in-law, Quintus Marcius Rex (*cos.* 68 BC), the governor of Cilicia. Marcius, who intensely disliked Lucullus and was more than happy to show his contempt for him, had given the young mutineer the command of a war fleet. It was while out on patrol with this fleet that Clodius had been seized. It seems that abduction by pirates had become something of an occupational hazard for young Roman aristocrats.

Khorvirap Monastery, Armenia, with Mount Ararat (5,165m) in the distance. The river Arax (Araxes) flows close by, while a nearby hill is the location of ancient Artashat (Artaxata), found in 185 BC by Artashes (Artaxias). The first king of Armenia was said to have chosen this site on the advice of Hannibal. It was outside Artaxata that Tigranes (r. 95–55 BC), who had not assumed the Achaemenid title 'king of kings', kowtowed to Pompey and got his throne back, but not much else. His kingdom was to become a Roman dependency, and his son and heir a hostage in Rome. (Andrew Behesnilian)

The imperial proconsul

Following the successful conclusion of the pirate war, Pompey spent the winter with the bulk of his army in Cilicia. At the beginning of 66 BC the *lex Manilia*, the tribunician bill of Caius Manilius, granted Pompey command of the war effort against Mithridates. The majority of the Senate, recognising a frontrunner when they saw one, had abandoned their qualms and voted this time to award Pompey further and even more unprecedented powers. Not only was he to command the largest force ever sent to the east, but he was allowed to make war or peace without direct reference to the Senate, the obvious intention being that he should defeat Mithridates once and for all. By contrast, Lucullus, whose reputation was now in tatters, was left with nothing. At the time it seemed logical to grant Pompey the mission against the Pontic king, and amongst the backers of the law was Cicero, now a praetor, who was to support Pompey loyally in the years to follow.

Remarkable as it may seem, this was the occasion of Cicero's first public speech. In his address in favour of Manilius' law, Cicero was to declare with the finely timed rhetoric of his craft that Pompey possessed in abundance the four chief attributes of a great general, namely 'military knowledge, courage, authority and good luck' (*de imperio Cnaeo Pompeii* 28) – by all accounts, Pompey was born with a good share of the latter. Though born in the same year as Pompey, Cicero was practically without military experience – he had served for a very short time in the army of Pompey's father during the Social War (Cic. *Phil.* 12.27) – and was anything but a soldier. Yet his inaugural speech shows him eloquently committed in his support of Pompey, faithfully

Pompey's commands: the east, 66–62 BC

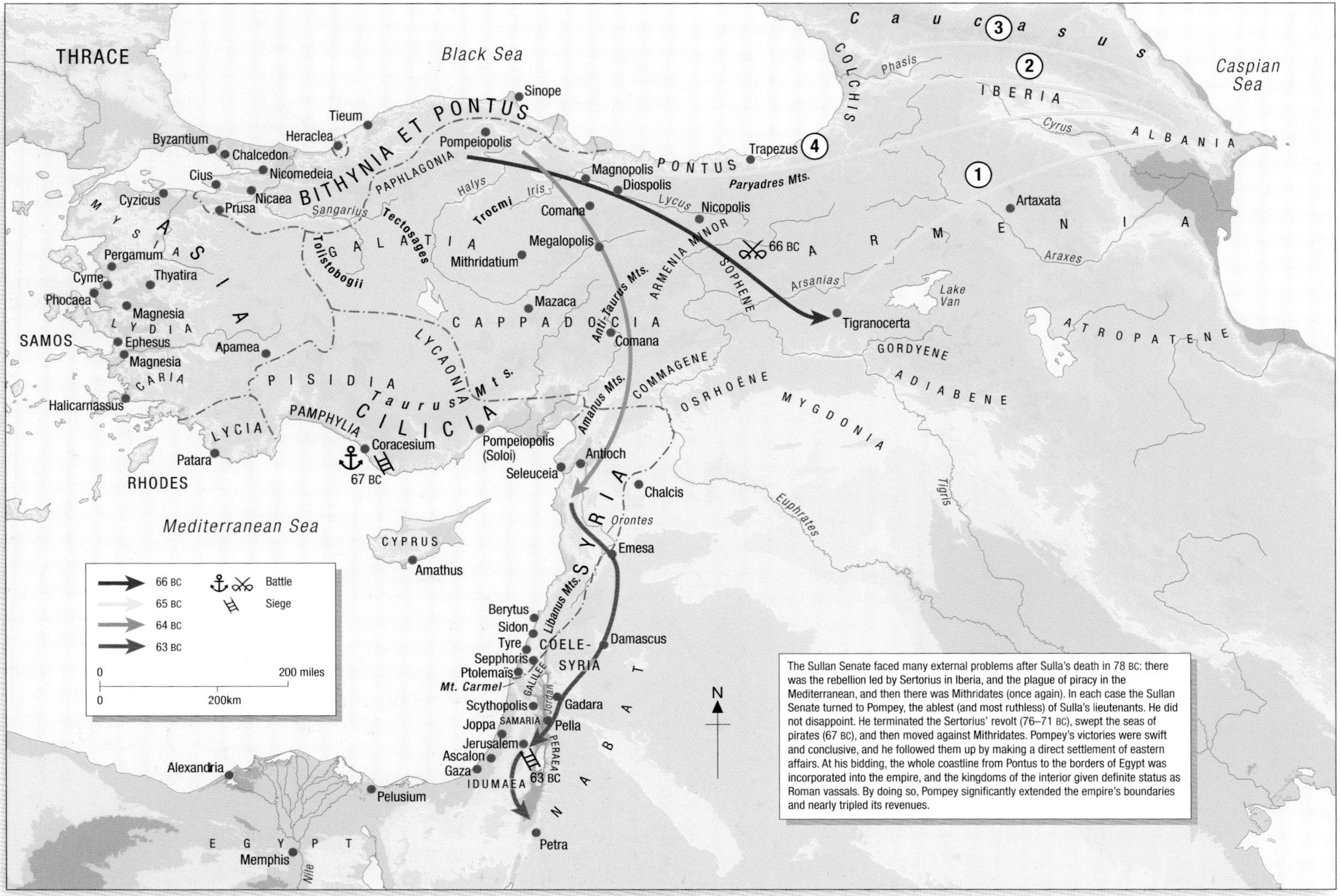

Battle
Siege

66 BC
65 BC
64 BC
63 BC

200 miles
200km

27

The Euphrates near the fortress of Halabiyeh, Syria. The site dates back to the Assyrian and Palmyrene periods. Farhad III (Phraates, r. 70–57 BC), the Parthian king, sent an envoy to Pompey bearing a message suggesting that the Euphrates should be considered the boundary between his empire (right bank) and that of the Romans (left bank). At the time not much was known about the 'effeminate' Parthians; such ignorance was to spectacularly change when Crassus crossed the Euphrates in the spring of 53 BC. (Bertramz)

reflecting the moderate opinion of the day. Fundamentally, at all times, Cicero himself was a moderate, opposed both to reaction and revolution.

With all the backbreaking groundwork already done by the luckless Lucullus, Pompey swiftly defeated Mithridates in his first year of operations. Making full use of his naval strength, Pompey sent his ships to guard the Asiatic coast from Syria to the Bosporus, a precaution against any attack on his rear by the Pontic navy. He then left his Cilician base to confront Mithridates in the north. The army he took with him was not large, being only as much as he needed, for he had already by adroit diplomacy managed to involve Tigranes against the Parthians, and the Pontic king was conveniently isolated.

Mithridates encamped at first in a strong mountain fastness, in a part of his kingdom known as Lesser Armenia, but retreated to a less secure position as a result of water shortage. Pompey occupied the stronghold thus vacated, deduced from the vegetation that water existed at no great depth and successfully dug wells. Subsequently, however, despite Pompey's engineering efforts to cut him off, Mithridates slipped away eastward with a still substantial army. Pompey pursued him as far as the upper reaches of the Euphrates, and an engagement was fought there by moonlight. The low moon behind the Romans cast long shadows ahead of them and played havoc with Pontic missile fire. What followed is quickly told. Gripped by panic, Mithridates' army turned and ran (Front. *Strat.* 2.1.12, Plut. *Pomp.* 32).

Again, the crafty king escaped and fled to the northernmost part of his realm in the Crimea, taking the landward route around the eastern shore of the Black Sea in order to avoid the Roman fleet patrolling its waters. Meanwhile, Pompey pushed on to Artaxata, where Tigranes wisely negotiated a surrender, and on payment of 6,000 talents and capitulation of his conquests, was reinstated by Pompey as a 'friend of the Roman people' to hold Armenia as a docile buffer state. Soon afterwards, Pompey was asked by the Parthian king, whom he had induced to attack Tigranes by the promise of territory, to recognize the Euphrates as 'the boundary between his empire and that of the Romans'. Pompey made the ominously Delphic response that the boundary 'adopted would be a just one' (Plut. *Pomp.* 33.6).

The mountainous landscape of Svaneti, in north-western Georgia, with the Greater Caucasus in the background. Historically, the western portion of Georgia was known as Colchis while the eastern plateau was called Iberia. On the defeat of Mithridates in 65 BC, the kingdom of Colchis was occupied by Pompey, who installed Aristarchos as a dynast (r. 65–47 BC), but the Roman presence he established in the kingdom of Iberia was not to be one of any permanence. (Petrusbarbygere)

As the Romans were soon to learn, the Parthians were troublesome only if disturbed on their own ground. As for the Pontic king, Pompey did not attempt to follow him northwards – the glittering but militarily irrelevant prize of Mithridates was not to be his concern – but found himself involved in gruelling warfare with the Iberi and Albani of the Caucasus, which was virgin territory for Roman arms.

Pompey was to spend the next three years reorganizing the east under Roman control. The whole coastline from Pontus to the borders of Egypt was incorporated into the empire, and the kingdoms of the interior were given definitive status as Roman vassals. In the north, not only Armenia, but Cimmerian Bosporus, Colchis and Iberia were added to the area under Roman suzerainty, which extended, in theory, as far as the Albani of the eastern Caucasus. This career of eastern conquest gained for Pompey a huge patronage, but it was pointed out that he was not, in fact, doing much campaigning against Mithridates. Pompey, however, had decided that Lucullus was wrong to follow the old king around his territories while his army grew ever more tired of the chase. Instead he made it diplomatically impossible for Mithridates to gather allies or find any place to rest. 'He declared', as Plutarch writes, 'that

General view of Mytilene port, looking north-north-east towards the Genoese castle. In the spring of 62 BC Pompey distributed lavish rewards to his soldiers and then set out in a rather leisurely fashion to return to Rome. Among the places he visited were Mytilene, the home of his personal chronicler and political agent Theophanes. The Greek city was granted its freedom as a compliment to its distinguished citizen (Vell. 2.18.1). In return, Mytilene was to pay honours and the appellation of saviour and benefactor not only to Pompey but also to the eloquent Theophanes. (Fields-Carré Collection)

Model of the Temple rebuilt by Herod, exhibited at the Israel Museum, Jerusalem. Despite internal discord between the partisans of the two contenders for the Jewish throne, Pompey was forced to besiege Jerusalem for three months before the city was taken with considerable slaughter. The moat on the north side of the Temple had been filled up by the Romans on a Sabbath, and in the fearful struggle that followed no fewer than 12,000 defenders are said to have perished. (Airely)

for Mithridates he was leaving behind a stronger opponent than himself – namely paucity' (*Pomp.* 39.1).

In the summer of 64 BC Pompey marched into Antioch. Antiochos, the 13th man of that name to have sat upon the Seleukid throne, and recently restored to it by Lucullus, fled into the desert, where he was ignominiously murdered by an Arab chieftain. Pompey dispatched the wrath of his kingdom and annexed Syria, declaring it a new province of the empire – probably as a bulwark against the Parthians. The following year, after abortive plans to make a comeback, Mithridates died in the Crimea.

In the meantime Pompey had headed south to campaign in a Iudaea torn by civil war. There he laid siege to Jerusalem, and after three months took it by storm. The first man over the walls in the final assault was Faustus Cornelius Sulla, the dictator's son. On entering the city Pompey and his senior officers went into the holy of holies within the Temple of Jerusalem, following the Roman urge to be the first to do anything, but out of respect took nothing from it (Josephus *Antiquitates Iudaicae* 14.29–79, *Bellum Iudaicum* 1.127–157). After settling the affairs of Jerusalem, Pompey created a list of dependent minor principalities including Emesa, Ituraea, Iudaea and the extensive, if sparsely populated, kingdom of the Nabataean Arabs, whose capital was at rose-red Petra.

Siege of Jerusalem, summer 63 BC: Pompey vs. the Sadducees

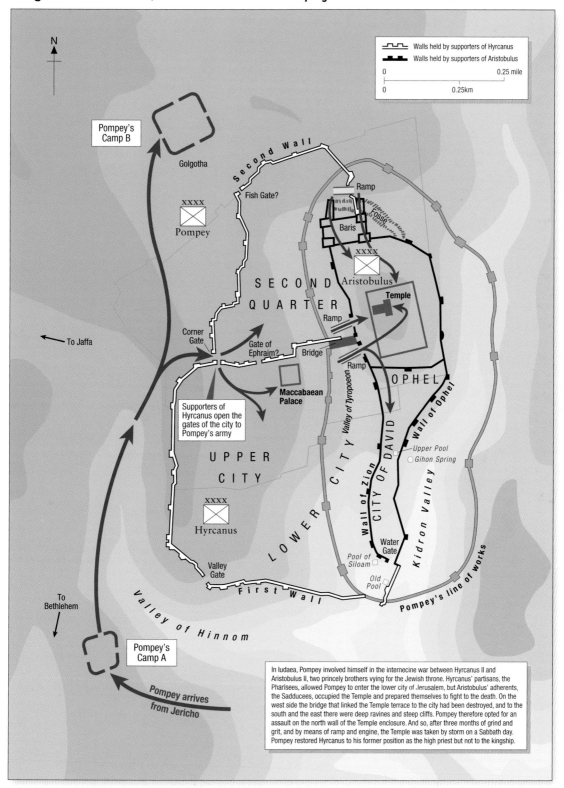

In Iudaea, Pompey involved himself in the internecine war between Hyrcanus II and Aristobulus II, two princely brothers vying for the Jewish throne. Hyrcanus' partisans, the Pharisees, allowed Pompey to enter the lower city of Jerusalem, but Aristobulus' adherents, the Sadducees, occupied the Temple and prepared themselves to fight to the death. On the west side the bridge that linked the Temple terrace to the city had been destroyed, and to the south and the east there were deep ravines and steep cliffs. Pompey therefore opted for an assault on the north wall of the Temple enclosure. And so, after three months of grind and grit, and by means of ramp and engine, the Temple was taken by storm on a Sabbath day. Pompey restored Hyrcanus to his former position as the high priest but not to the kingship.

Pompey's hard-hitting campaign against the Mediterranean pirates demonstrated that he had genuine talents as an organizer and an administrator, which was something of a surprise, for in his youth he had been dynamic, violent and unprincipled, a dashing heads-down fighter, and no man to put in charge of an important command. Yet as a consular commander, Pompey showed none of the recklessness for which he had been known as a young man in Sicily, Africa and Iberia. For Pompey, unlike his rival in the glory game Caesar, there were to be no more heroics, no more glorious victories at the cost of mounds of glorious dead.

Flat-baked clay plaque (London, British Museum, inv. 91908) bearing a Parthian cataphract, dated from the 3rd or 2nd century BC. Cataphracts typically had scale or lamellar armour for both horse and rider, and were armed with a heavy spear some 3.65m in length and held two-handed without a shield. A weapon for shock action, it was driven home with the full thrust of the body behind it. The Romans came to know cataphracts during their wars in the Hellenistic east, but they remained ineffective against legionaries, being defeated at Magnesia (190 BC) and Tigranocerta (69 BC). But when combined with horse archers, as at Carrhae (53 BC), it was the legionaries who came off worse. (World Imaging)

It was Pompey's eastern campaigns that were to stand as his greatest achievements, while the settlement that followed was a testament to his genius for organization. These unprecedented victories had brought Rome vast accessions of territory, as well as a host of new dependent allies and a huge influx of treasure and revenue. Rome knew no limit or scruple and, as Cicero tells us, 'the essential significance, surely, of those eulogistic words inscribed upon the monuments of our greatest generals, "he extended the boundaries of the empire", is that he had extended them by taking territory from someone else' (*rep.* 3.24). And naturally such belligerent imperialism not only brought territories and taxes, but slaves and spoils too. Under the Republic conquests were often very bloody – a body count of 5,000 qualified a general for a triumph back in Rome – and were followed up by enslavement and pillage to defray the costs of the campaign, fill the yawning purse of the general and give his threadbare soldiers something to take home into civilian life. Although, like every Roman conqueror before him, Pompey exploited the lands he conquered, nevertheless, he gave their people peace such as they had not enjoyed since the fall of the Persian Empire.

In a sense, Pompey personified Roman imperialism, where absolute destruction was followed by the construction of stable empire and the rule of law. It also, not coincidentally, raised him to a pinnacle of glory and wealth. The client-rulers who swelled the train of Rome also swelled his own. He received extraordinary honours from the communities of the east as 'saviour and benefactor of the people and of all Asia, guardian of land and sea' (*ILS* 9459). There was an obvious precedent for all this. As the elder Pliny later wrote, Pompey's victories 'equalled in brilliance the exploits of Alexander the Great'. Without a doubt, so Pliny continues, the proudest boast of our Roman Alexander would be that 'he found Asia on the rim of Rome's possessions, and left it in the centre' (*HN* 7.95, 99). Thus the notion of taking Roman

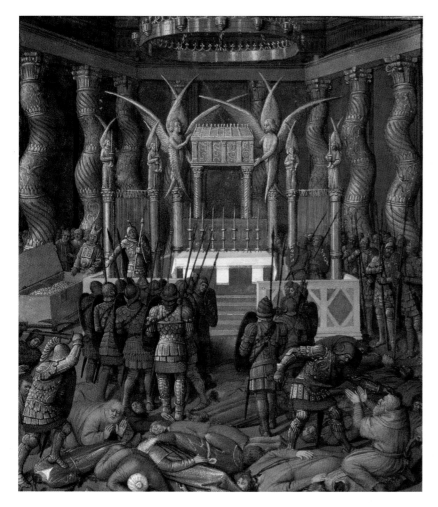

Desecration of the Temple of Jerusalem in 63 BC by Pompey and his soldiers (Paris, Bibliothèque Nationale, Ms Fr 247 f.293) by Jean Fouquet (c.1470, vellum). To the great sorrow of the Jews, Pompey penetrated into their innermost sanctuary. But this desecration of the Temple was more through curiosity than covetousness – its great treasures were to be carted off by Crassus a few years later. (Bridgeman Art Library)

dominion to 'the ends of the earth' (*ultimas terrarum fines*) reaches its climax with Pompey, who, we are told, 'wanted to extend his conquests to the ocean that surrounds the world on all sides' (Plut. *Pomp.* 38.2).

On a darker note, Pompey's activities went beyond any brief given to him by Rome. The settlement of the east was his, not the Senate's. Pompey's power and influence rested not simply upon the *imperium* given by Rome, but on his personal influence, connections and patronage. In the final showdown with Caesar the east would provide Pompey with his most solid support.

OPPOSING COMMANDERS

During his long military career, which stretched over a period of four decades, Pompey faced some worthy opponents, foreign and Roman alike, the most notable being of course Caesar. However, Caesar I have dealt with in depth in Command 4: *Julius Caesar*, so here I shall discuss only Sertorius and Mithridates, two men who were significant in the unfolding drama of Pompey's extraordinary and lengthy career.

Quintus Sertorius (*c*.126–73 BC)

Quintus Sertorius does not get much space in the history books, but this rough, blunt and talented *novus homo* successfully maintained an open rebellion against the Sullan regime for nigh on a decade. Unquestionably brave, the young Sertorius had been wounded at Arausio (105 BC), the biggest calamity to Roman arms since Cannae. As one of the ten men said to have survived (Orosius 5.16.5), his escape from the disaster became the stuff of legend. Having lost his horse in the battle, Sertorius jumped into the broad and swift-flowing Rhône and swam across, though still 'in arms and breastplate' (Ammianus Marcellinus 24.6.7). Next serving under Marius against the migrating Germans, the Cimbri and the Teutones, along with certain Gaulish tribes, he had readily disguised himself as a Celt so as to spy out their intentions (Plut. *Sert.* 3.2). After the annihilation of the Teutones and Ambrones (102 BC), and then the Cimbri (101 BC), he fought in Iberia (97–92 BC), and, probably as a proquaestor, in the Social War (91–88 BC), during which he lost an eye (Plut. *Sert.* 4.2). Siding with Marius and Cinna, he did not hesitate to continue the struggle against Sulla even after all others had either been liquidated or gone to ground. He had an almost foolhardy and quixotic approach to danger.

In 81 BC Sertorius, serving as governor of Hispania Ulterior, was expelled by a pro-Sullan replacement. Seeking refuge in Mauretania, he managed to overcome its Sullan garrison. The following year Sertorius re-entered Iberia with a tiny army of 2,600 men, 'whom for honour's sake he called Romans, and a motley band of 700 Libyans' (Plut. *Sert.* 12.2), and opened a successful campaign against Sulla's henchmen there. An inspiring (if not brilliant) commander, by exploiting local backing he quickly established a Marian 'government in exile'. Acting as a proper Roman proconsul rather than an Iberian warlord leading some Iberians insurgents and a few Roman desperadoes, Sertorius had his own alternative senate and a readiness to recruit able local talent, whom he would encourage to learn Latin and proper Roman ways. He was to show how Iberians under proper leadership and discipline could hold Roman armies at bay.

In 79 BC Quintus Caecilius Metellus Pius (*cos.* 80 BC), son of the man who had successfully warred against Iugurtha, was sent to Iberia to expel Sertorius, but he turned out to be no match for Sertorius and suffered a number of reverses. The venerable Metellus Pius, after Sulla, was the foremost Roman of his day, a loyal servant of the oligarchy whose supremacy the dictator had laboured to re-establish. By the end of the following year Sertorius was master of much of the peninsula, with influence

Montefortino helmet (Bad Deutsch-Altenburg, Archaeological Museum Carnuntum). As the Roman army moved into the period of huge expansion following the Marian reforms, cheap and undecorated but functional helmets needed to be mass-produced. Legionaries, many of them the poorest members of society, no longer provided their own equipment, and were instead issued with standard-issue weapons, armour and clothing by the state. This low-cost helmet pattern gave good protection to the top of the head. It had hinged cheek-pieces, but only a stubby nape guard. (Matthias Kabel) extending into Gallia Transalpina. It was about this time that he was reinforced by Perperna, whom we last met fleeing Italy, and the remnants of the Marian rebels who had backed the renegade Lepidus. And so the Sullan oligarchy, greatly alarmed that Sertorius, like a second Hannibal, might attempt to invade Italy, once again granted Pompey an extraordinary command, that of a propraetor, to assist the proconsul Metellus Pius.

We have already dealt with the events outside Lauron, so we shall jump ahead to the spring of 75 BC when Sertorius took the offensive against Pompey. The two of them promptly engaged in a hot, scrambling fight somewhere along the river Sucro (Júcar), united, as Plutarch dryly remarks, by the mutual fear that the dangerous, if lethargic, Metellus Pius should arrive before the day was decided. Pompey had to be rescued by the man whose glory he had hoped to steal, for only the timely arrival of the proconsul prevented his complete and utter rout. 'If the old women had not arrived, I would have whipped the boy back to Rome', comments Sertorius sourly afterwards (Plut. *Sert.* 19.6, *Pomp.* 18.1).

Pompey, or 'Sulla's pupil' as Sertorius was said to have dubbed him (Plut. *Sert.* 18.4), was facing for the first time in his career a commander of real ability, albeit of the unconventional kind. Though driven by circumstances into a war against his own people, Sertorius turned out to be adept at leading irregular forces and exploiting a protean ability to disperse them in order to escape the clutches of larger enemy forces. Having served in Iberia before, he fully appreciated that even the most dangerous opponent could be defeated if gradually worn down in a series of small wars, for continuous pressure is more effective than mere brute force. In a country that was inhospitably rugged and with native troops that were swift in movement and skilful in concealment, Sertorius would cut supply lines, ambush convoys, harass foragers and eventually sap the resolve of those who survived (Plut. *Sert.* 10.2–3).

Sertorius would not have known the meaning of the words, but he had discovered the enormous effectiveness of something that would come to be called guerrilla warfare. Beyond anything else, he was following the basic guerrilla precepts of attacking when least expected and avoiding a general action, so as never to be drawn into a situation where he would have to gamble his cause in an unfavourable battle. By adopting unconventional warfare activities, Sertorius was implying that he would be content to harass the Romans at every opportunity, stealthily ambushing them and slicing as many as possible to pieces before vanishing as silently and surreptitiously as arriving. To demonstrate to his irregulars they should not risk all on one large-scale open-field encounter with the superior Roman army,

Terracotta statuette (London, British Museum, inv. WA 1972.2.29,1/ 135684) of a Parthian horse archer. Here we witness the brilliant riding skills, combined with the use of a composite bow short enough to fire in any direction from horseback, even straight backwards over the animal's rump: the celebrated 'Parthian shot'. While riding away from an enemy, in either a real or feigned retreat, a Parthian could turn back in the saddle and fire arrows at his pursuers. This was achieved by twisting the torso while simultaneously drawing the bow, and then firing to the rear, all in one fluid motion. (Fields-Carré Collection)

Battle of the Sucro, spring 75 BC: Pompey vs. Sertorius

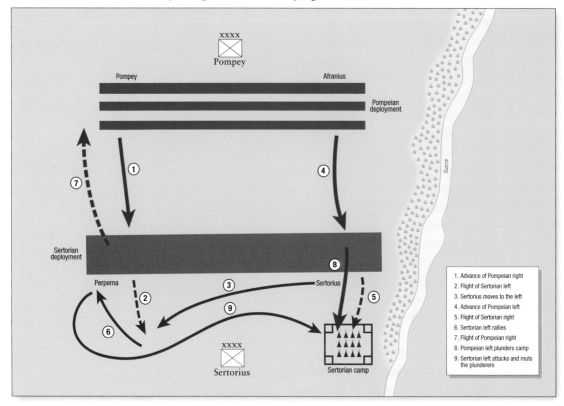

Sertorius arranged for two horses, one run-down and the other robust, to be brought before them, and ordered a strong man to pull the tail off the nag at a stroke, which was impossible. He then had a weak man pull the hairs from the tail of the stallion one by one (Val. Max. 7.3.6, Front. *Strat.* 1.10.1, Pliny *Epistulae* 3.9.11), thus demonstrating his principle of continuous harassment being the most effective way to defeat the enemy, rather than one decisive engagement.

Late in 75 BC, Sertorius hosted an embassy from Mithridates of Pontus. Seemingly, in return for warships and money, Sertorius was prepared to concede not only Bithynia and Cappadocia but also the Roman province of Asia (App. *Mith.* §68). Sertorius had put the matter before his senate and the general consensus of opinion was that the loss of territory not under their control was a small price to pay for aid, though Plutarch (*Sert.* 23.4–5) expressly denies that Sertorius agreed to give up the Roman province. Whether he did or not (cf. Spann 1987: 101), he did send military advisers to organize and train the Pontic army in Roman fighting methods (App. *Mith.* §77, Orosius 6.2.12, Plut. *Lucull.* 8.5, 12.5, cf. 7.4).

Insurgent that he was, when circumstances required, Sertorius did not hesitate to offer pitched battle, as we saw at the Sucro. He thus taught Pompey several sharp lessons, especially in their early encounters, and Pompey was to learn from his mistakes, quickly maturing as a commander.

Celtiberian bronze fibula (Madrid, Museo Arqueológico Nacional, inv. 22925) representing a horseman, dating from the 3rd or 2nd century BC. Under the horse's head there hangs a lopped-off head, undoubtedly taken in combat. Both Pompey and Caesar employed in their armies contingents of Iberian horse, which were of excellent quality and were trained and equipped to fight *en masse*. (Luis García)

Yet the Iberian war revealed that Pompey could be outmatched on the battlefield by a general of ability. In the end, Pompey, by campaigning with more circumspection and operating in concert with Metellus Pius, gradually backed his wily mentor into a corner. Sertorius' victories, the lifeblood of any guerrilla leader, became less frequent, and his supporters, both Roman and Iberian, began to waver in their support, while he himself abandoned his previously frugal habits and turned to alcohol and women, or so we are told (App. *BC* 1.113, Diodoros 37.22a).

In the mid-to-late summer of 73 BC a conspiracy of senior Marian officers headed by the noble and proud Perperna, who resented a mere ex-praetor being his commander and decided that he could do better, resulted in Sertorius' assassination during a drunken dinner party (Sall. *Hist.* 3.83). Perperna, ultimately of Etruscan origin was nevertheless a Roman and a noble (Vell. 2.30.1), whose father and grandfather had been consuls. He obviously possessed pride greatly in excess of his actual ability, for his military record to date was an unbroken string of defeats, several of them inflicted by Pompey himself. In any case, within days of his sordid *coup d'état*, Perperna, who was no adroit guerrilla fighter like Sertorius, was lured into a classic Sertorian ambush, taken prisoner and executed out of hand (Plut. *Pomp.* 20.3, *Sert.* 27.3).

By the following year Pompey had brought the Iberian conflict to a successful conclusion, and he commemorated it with a trophy in the Pyrenees, topped by his own statue and inscribed to say that he had conquered no less than 876 towns from the Alps to the boundaries of Hispania Ulterior (Sall. *Hist.* 3.89, Strabo 3.4.1, 7, 9, 4.1.3, Plin. *HN* 7.27.1, 37.6.3, Dio 41.24.3, Flor. 2.10.9). We are perhaps looking here at an early example of his self-publicity outrunning his real achievements. If Pliny adds innocently that Pompey made no mention of Sertorius on his hyperbolic memorial, it is Florus who knows the reason why, for Pompey desired the conflict to be considered a foreign war rather than a civil one, so that he might celebrate a triumph.

There was no such monument for Sertorius, not even a marked grave. In fact, the role of Sertorius receives little attention in the histories of the Republic, while the man himself slipped quietly into history to be little remembered. But that oversight does not diminish how he directly influenced Pompey's career. Sertorius' situation prevented him from reaching the front rank of those Roman commanders military history has chosen to commemorate, leaving him overshadowed by Pompey who, in the apt words of Spann, 'survived and stepped over Sertorius to greatness' (1987: 151).

Mithridates VI, Eupator of Pontus (r. *c.*113–65 BC)

The kingdom of Pontus had once been an out-of-the-way satrapy of the Achaemenid Persian Empire, but after the time of Alexander the Great its rulers had established themselves as an independent dynasty. The population may have contained Greek, Thracian, Scythian and Celtic elements, but it was dominated by a well-established Iranian aristocracy, and its kings adopted, or at any rate affected, Greek culture. The sixth Mithridates (to use the Greek spelling of his name, which in Old Persian was *Mithradatha*, 'gift of Mithra'), with whom we are concerned, had presented himself as a champion of Greek civilization, and in this role he had given military protection to the Greek states dotted along the northern shores of the Black Sea, firmly imposing his authority in this region. As a result he had ready access to fertile grain-growing lands and to the resources of wealthy Greek maritime states, including a substantial navy. Mithridates, a cunning opportunist, would wage a series of wars against the Romans in an effort to drive them from Asia and Greece.

Rome had acquired a toehold in Anatolia, and the region along the Ionian coast was soon transformed into the province of Asia, a province now separated from the Pontic kingdom by only a thin array of pliant Roman allies. With just a token force in Asia, Roman commanders prior to Pompey had not been able to face Mithridates directly, so they had encouraged their local allies to act as proxies and police Pontus. The scheme proved disastrous. In 98 BC, despite Marius having warned him to curb his territorial ambitions, Mithridates invaded Cappadocia, a territory to which he had some territorial claim. Two years later, the Senate sent Sulla east as propraetor to Cilicia on the southern coast of Anatolia. He had apparently gone there to check

Marble portrait of Mithridates VI Eupator (Paris, musée du Louvre, inv. Ma 2321) in lion *exuviae*, thereby identifying himself as a reincarnation of the divine Herakles and the successor of the world-conquering Alexander the Great. Of all the enemies of Rome, Mithridates lasted the longest, having fought Sulla, Lucullus and Pompey. In 63 BC, the old king, abandoned by all, died by his own hand after defying the might of Rome for almost three decades. He would be remembered as a ruler of near-mythical proportions. (Fields-Carré Collection)

piracy, a perennially favourite pastime of the Cilicians, but he had also managed to install Ariobarzanes, who was a Roman friend, on the throne of Cappadocia. Mithridates had already been told to give up that kingdom and Paphlagonia as well, but the Senate's command had not, by itself, proven enough. Sulla had marched off on his mission using only local levies. During his little campaign, which he commanded with his usual skill, Sulla's forces had clashed with those of Tigranes II, king of Armenia. While nothing came of it directly, Tigranes threw his lot in with Mithridates: he married his daughter.

In 91 BC Mithridates once again appeared at the head of a massive, westward-moving army. He seized Cappadocia for a second time, as well as Bithynia, with the aid of his son-in-law Tigranes, and the Senate, once again, ordered him out. Two years later Manius Aquillius, Marius' old comrade-in-arms during the war against the northern tribes and his colleague as consul in 101 BC, was eventually despatched east by the Senate to confront Mithridates and drive him back to his own territories. Aquillius joined local levies to the troops of Lucius Cassius, proconsul of Asia, and threw Mithridates out of Cappadocia and Bithynia, installing Nikomedes IV as the new ruler of Bithynia. However, Aquillius went beyond his brief and extorted a large sum from Nikomedes in exchange for the liberation of his kingdom, which, manifestly, he could not pay. Therefore, under pressure from the Roman general, the Bithynian king was encouraged to raid across the border into Pontic territory. Mithridates lodged a formal complaint with the Senate.

A diplomatic nicety observed, Mithridates then exploited the foray of debt-ridden Nikomedes by invading his kingdom (First Mithridatic War, 89–85 BC). Defeating the Roman forces four times in quick succession, he not only gained Bithynia, Phrygia, Mysia, Lycia, Pamphylia, Ionia and Cappadocia, but the Roman province of Asia too, which he started to dismantle. On the king's orders, the local authorities in every city of the province rounded up and put to death all resident Italians – men, women and children – in a single day (App. *Mith.* §§85–91). Plutarch (*Sulla* 24.4) says that 150,000 were killed, but even if we lower the figure to the 80,000 given by other sources, this calculated atrocity had a staggering impact. To crown this stunning reversal, Aquillius fell into the hands of the vengeful king, who had him paraded on an ass and then executed by the theatrical expedient of pouring molten gold down his throat as a punishment for his rapacity.

It appears that Mithridates was no ordinary enemy of Rome. Persecuted by his wicked mother as a child, the young prince had been forced to take refuge in the mountains of north-eastern Anatolia. Here, according to a

Silver tetradrachm of Mithridates VI Eupator (London, British Museum), from around 75 BC, showing the youthful features of Alexander. Whereas his ancestors had used philhellenism as a means of attaining respectability and acceptance in the Hellenistic east, Mithridates used it as an overt political tool. Posing as a champion of Greek civilization, Mithridates would wage a series of wars with the 'barbarian' Romans in an effort to drive them from Asia and Greece. By doing so he became the 'great liberator' of the Greek world. (PHGCOM)

The Pontic Mountains near Trabzon. These mountains divided the kingdom of Pontus into two distinct areas, the coastal region hugging the Black Sea and the mountainous inland area. This division was also cultural, the coast being mainly Greek and nautical, and the interior occupied by Cappadocians and Paphlagonians ruled by an Iranian aristocracy. Mithridates VI Eupator would be the last ruler of this Hellenistic kingdom. (Aleksafi)

biography that reads almost like a fairy tale, he lived in the wilds for seven years, outrunning deer and outfighting lions, or so it was said. Nervous that his mother might still have him murdered, Mithridates developed a morbid fascination with toxicology, dining daily on smidgens of poisons and antidotes to confer immunity when his body encountered the toxin again. But in time the prince, terrible and splendid, emerged from the wilderness with an army of supporters, killed his mother, and then, just for good measure, his usurping brother and sister too. Of course, such legends are partly the product of mythologizing, especially by Roman authors; for Mithridates became in the collective psyche of the Romans an archetypal enemy alongside such perennial *bêtes noires* as Brennos and Hannibal.

Following his spectacular victories, Mithridates crossed the Aegean into Greece, where he routed yet another Roman army and occupied Athens. Exploiting his European toehold was difficult. His forces were constantly harassed by Roman troops, now reinforced by the legions of Sulla, and the Greek cities had come to see the erstwhile liberator as little better than the Romans. Mithridates, a consummate politician, knew when the game was up, and quickly concluded a peace agreement with Sulla: he renounced his conquests and agreed to pay an indemnity for disturbing the peace. That was hardly the end, however. Beaten he may have been, but Mithridates still sat on the throne of Pontus – practically a guarantee of future war. What followed was a series of small but bloody wars, again pitting Mithridates against his neighbours and, in turn, against Rome.

Within a few years, Rome at last reached the end of its tether. The Senate once again invested ultimate military authority in Pompey. The new

Pompey's commands: civil war, 49–48 BC

Caesar's mounting reputation cast a dismal shadow over Pompey's, and the Senate, having no doubt that Pompey could handle his rival in the glory game, and that they could handle him in the political one, quickly reminded Pompey that it was his republican duty to protect the constitution. However, Caesar was too fleet of foot for the uneasy coalition of Pompeians and republicans, and seized Italy in a lightning campaign. Before the year was out he held the Pompeian stronghold of Iberia too (49 BC). The following year, at Pharsalus, Caesar won a decisive victory over the army Pompey had recruited by stripping the eastern provinces bare of legions.

Legend:

- ⊠ (x) Pompey's legions, January 49 BC
- ⊠ (x) Caesar's legions, January 49 BC
- ⫿⫿ Siege (with date)
- ⚔ Battle (with date)

0 — 200 miles
0 — 200 km

GALLIA COMATA

GALLIA CISALPINA

GALLIA TRANSALPINA

ILLYRICUM

Alps

Pyrenees

Liger

Danubius

Rhodanus

Padus

Rubicon

Iberus

Adriatic Sea

Ionian Sea

Mediterranean Sea

Aquileia

legio XIII — Caesar

Ravenna

Ariminum

Arretium

Corfinium — ⫿⫿ 49 BC

Rome

Capua

Ahenobarbus ⊠

legiones I and III — Pompey ⊠ x 2

Brundisium

Antony March 48 BC

Pompey March 49 BC

Caesar January 48 BC

Nymphaeum ⫿⫿ 48 BC

Dyrrhachium

Apollonia

Oricum

Pharsalus ⚔ 48 BC

legiones VI–XII and XIIII ⊠ x 8

legiones VIII and XI

legiones VI, VII, VIIII, X, XI and XIIII

Massilia ⫿⫿ 49 BC

Narbo

Ilerda ⚔ 49 BC

Petreius Afranius ⊠ x 7

N

41

campaign against Mithridates was swift. As in the past, the king staged a strategic retreat, like the Pied Piper of Hamelin attempting to lure the Roman legions from the flat lands into rugged territory and there wear them down. Mithridates, unlike the Romans, placed as much emphasis on backward movement as he did on forward. He believed that a calculated withdrawal gave him an option of a forward movement in the future. But Pompey refused to take the bait. When Mithridates was bundled out of Pontus, fleeing to the Caucasus, Pompey turned his attention to Armenia, quickly subjugating the king's ally, Tigranes. He then marched along the southern coast of the Black Sea, conquering cities that had earlier fallen to Mithridates and invading the Pontic kingdom itself.

In the meantime, the wily king had made good his escape, riding north among the Caucasian tribes and avoiding the coast, which was patrolled by Roman ships. He finally arrived at Panticapaeum (Ketch), where he had installed one of his sons as ruler of the Crimea. With most of Pontus now in his grip, Pompey turned his attention to quelling rebellions elsewhere, leaving the exiled king to brood among the barbarians of the north.

In his Crimean redoubt, Mithridates was plotting his Pontic comeback. As power-hungry and ruthless as ever, he drew up an elaborate scheme to raise a new army among the Scythians and Getae, march round the Black Sea and up the Danube, and, with the assistance of some Gauls, cross the Alps and race down through Italy to attack Rome itself (Dio 37.11.1, App. *Mith.* §102, §109). This time, however, his audacious aims overreached his ageing abilities. Although he had initially been welcomed as a liberator, in time he had come to seem little more than a tyrant, exacting the same tribute for himself that he had warned local potentates they would be required to pay under Roman authority. Mutinies broke out among his own soldiers, and his fifth son, Pharnaces, persuaded the officers to crown him king in his father's place. Realizing that his throne was lost, Mithridates attempted suicide by drinking poison. When it failed to take effect, in desperation he tried to stab himself. In the end, a merciful Gaul in his retinue dispatched him with his sword (App. *Mith.* §111). Indomitable to the bitter end, he had warred against Rome for 24 years.

The traitorous Pharnaces quickly sent Pompey a token of goodwill and friendship: the body of his father. Pompey pronounced him the greatest adversary that Rome had encountered in the east and buried him in a specially built mausoleum in Sinope. After a few mopping-up operations,

Pompey reorganized the newly acquired lands, and Pontus was made part of the Roman province of Bithynia-and-Pontus. As a final, fascinating note, Mithridates' scrolls on toxins and antidotes also became the property of Rome, and in due course came into the hands of the greatest physician of antiquity, Galen.

WHEN WAR IS DONE

Goethe once defined true genius as knowing when to stop. In Pompey's later years his mind was in decline, very much like the setting sun – the size remaining, but without the force. Genius can be baffling too. It is certainly not the product of intelligence, learning, training or discipline, but is instead an intuitive and spontaneous display of power that reasoning can never really fathom. All the same, we can enlist the aid of the Greek poet Archilochus, who once said, 'the fox knows many things, the hedgehog one great thing'. At a time when the Republic was quickly slipping into morbidity, the fox was Caesar and the hedgehog was Pompey, with his one massive, all-encompassing passion.

Pompey had achieved the kind of eminence that attracts lethal envy and arouses the suspicions of any traditionalists wary of new-made military grandees, taking for himself the power that had long been vested in their aristocratic oligarchy. Yet more than ever, with Caesar rapping at the door, the Senate needed to bind Pompey to its interests. It is a curious feature of their relationship that, two decades after their strange courtship had begun, no permanent understanding had been reached. Each desired the other, and each needed the other, but they had never moved beyond diffidence and mutual suspicion. This state of affairs was largely inevitable through the interaction of the snobbish suspicions of the stale Senate and the brash overconfidence of the parvenu Pompey.

The city walls of Lucca, on the site of ancient Luca in Etruria. It was here in mid-April 56 BC that the so-called conference took place between the 'big three' in order to settle their supposed differences and ordain the course of future political events. In truth, it was meeting just between two of the dynasts, Pompey and Caesar, the latter looking after the interests of the third, Crassus. According to an aside from Cicero (*fam*. 1.9.5), a man surely in the know, Caesar had previously met with Crassus at Ravenna. (Fototeca ENIT)

The Rubicon, flowing through Bellaria-Igea Marina, Emilia-Romagna. A minor river even for the Romans, the Rubicon is famous of course for Caesar's predawn crossing. With this step, Caesar passed a point of no return. For Pompey, on the other hand, it was to be the beginning of the end. (Stefano Bolognini)

Nothing illustrates this better than the occasion when Pompey appeared uniformed, armed and belligerent, and, with his usual fatal facility for creating a phrase that would be long remembered, he hubristically announced that 'I have only to stamp my foot upon the ground [of Italy], and there will rise armies of infantry and armies of cavalry' (Plut. *Pomp.* 57.5). Arrogant and inclined to over-dramatization – the beast can never get rid of its spots – Pompey was obviously buoyed up by his past successes and his own conceited self-confidence, but, as he was soon to find out, times had changed.

Now Caesar operated on the theory that an army's function is to get at the enemy in the speediest possible way and destroy him, and the night he crossed the Rubicon things began to hum. Pompey had been wrong: the people of Italy, apparently indifferent to the threat to senatorial rights and their own apparent liberties, let Caesar pass. This fact spoke volumes. In the event, a shortage of manpower forced Pompey to withdraw across the Adriatic without a fight, and stamp for his support there. From our present vantage point in time, we can assure ourselves that it was not the best judgement of his career. Pompey was now the prisoner of his own strategy: men thought that he had run away from Italy, and his self-respect and credibility as the generalissimo of the Republic demanded that he should fight his way back. After all, Pompey, for all his stark magnificence, was still a republican.

As we know, members of the republican aristocracy were constantly competing among themselves for military glory, and, of course, the economic rewards that accompanied it. As the stakes got higher in the late Republic, so the competition became more intense and more destructive to the political order. Pompey's career was extraordinary only in the sense that it represented, in an exaggerated form, the inherent contradictions of city-state politics played out on a Mediterranean-wide stage. Pompey was

The Cathedral of La Seu Vella, La Suda hill, Lérida (Catalan *Lleida*). This rocky eminence is the site of ancient Ilerda, the chief settlement of the Iberian Ilergetes, and its commanding position on the right bank of the Sicoris (Segre) induced the Pompeian legates, Afranius and Petreius, to make it the key of their defence against Caesar. (Hector Blanco de Frutos)

a successful soldier who undoubtedly aspired to the supremacy once held by Sulla. He had thrice been consul – on the third occasion, in 52 BC, for some months without a colleague – yet, notwithstanding his apparent power, his stiff formality stirred no exuberance and his political wavering made him generally mistrusted. Even so, we should not underestimate the man as many of his contemporaries did (e.g. Cic. *fam.* 8.1.3). By superb skill and timing he had risen from his lawless beginnings as a warlord of Picenum to a constitutional pre-eminence in which he could discard the use of naked force and still pose as the defender of the Republic. As Sallust said of him, he was 'moderate in everything but in seeking domination' (*Hist.* 2 fr. 14 Maurenbrecher). This is of course a Caesarian view, but it is also the simple truth. Had Pompey won Pharsalus, the Republic could hardly have endured.

Yet compared with Caesar, Pompey was at a serious disadvantage; he was a superannuated man living on his past fame. Whereas Caesar had spent all but one of the last nine years at war, Pompey had last seen active service

Durrës (ancient Dyrrhachium), Albania, with the palace of Zog, King of the Albanians (r. 1928–39), up on the hilltop. Pompey's strategy was to use the vast resources of the east to blockade and if need be to reconquer Italy. Caesar, however, sailing outside the normal sailing season, surprised Pompey and narrowly missed capturing the great trading port of Dyrrhachium, then serving as an all-important supply dump for the gathering Pompeian forces. (A. Dombrowski)

Pharsalus owes its place in military history to the Caesarian propaganda that hailed it as a major victory, as well as Caesar's own self-promotion, since it cemented Caesar's ascendancy and left the Republic an empty shell. Here we see the central plain of Thessaly north-west of modern Fársala. The battle itself was fought on the north bank of the Enipeus (today's Enipéas), which flows just north of the city. (Fields-Carré Collection)

in 62 BC, since when his prestige had sunk. Moreover, as a servant of the Senate he lacked absolute command, being as it was divided between the Pompeians and the diehard *optimates* led by Rome's leading exponent of Stoicism, Cato, who, according to Caesar, complained that Pompey had betrayed the Republic by not making better preparations for war. So his position as generalissimo was undermined by senators who prodded him into action that he might otherwise have delayed or not even have taken, and, added to this, he was saddled with two apathetic and dawdling consuls. Unity of command, Napoleon would state with absolute conviction, was 'the first necessity of war' (*Correspondance*, vol. XXXI, p. 418, note 40).

In his prime Pompey had been solid, sensible and thorough rather than nimble-witted or inspirational. He had worked hard, trained his men well and looked after them, and given clear orders. He had gained their allegiance by proven leadership and the odd promise, but never by way of high-flown phrases or florid speeches. Pompey was no orator. He did not have the facility of a Cato or a Caesar to articulate the words that inspired men. We catch a glimmer of this when Pompey addresses his soldiers in Epeiros: 'I have not abandoned, and would not abandon, the struggle on your behalf and in your company. As general and soldier, I offer myself to you' (App. *BC* 2.51). It was a calculated act of man management, and it had the desired effect of raising morale and generally improving the standard of discipline – in both respects there was undoubtedly room for improvement. In spite of lacking the ability to fire men up with brave talk, Pompey knew what connecting with his soldiers could do for morale, namely by motivating them to follow him into battle and inspiring them by building up their self-confidence. Pompey had an admirable ability to instil a fighting spirit in his men.

Pharsalus, the final battle

A major task of an ancient general was to draw up his battle line and issue relevant orders for pre-planned moves to be executed when battle was joined. Before battle, Pompey would sketch out a plan that was always sound, but he did not seem to have the knack to modify it according to circumstances. At Pharsalus he had the advantage in cavalry and was so confident that his 7,000 or so horsemen could carry the day that he seems to have almost held off his legionaries. His plan was to place all his cavalry on his left flank, where they would rout their opponents and then swing in behind Caesar's legions (particularly his favourite, the formidable *legio X*) and destroy them. But Caesar, immediately seeing through Pompey's plan, stripped his third line of six cohorts and posted them on his right to form a fourth line, invisible to the enemy. It was a brilliant *mise en scène*, the perfect deception: when the cavalry attacked and routed Caesar's heavily outnumbered horsemen, these cohorts waited until they were given the signal and then attacked so vigorously that Pompey's cavalry, startled and rattled, scattered to the four winds, as swift to fly as to advance. After cutting down some archers and slingers, the cohorts then swiftly swung in behind Pompey's main infantry line, arriving there like a bolt from the blue, and initiated the destruction of his legions. Quality of troops was of greater value than quantity, and Caesar actually credited his victory to these six cohorts (*BC* 3.94.4). Pompey, seeing the failure of his plan, was demoralized and beaten. The battle of Pharsalus was not Pompey's finest hour as a commander.

On the day, Caesar had out-gunned Pompey through a realistic appraisal of the circumstances that allowed him take advantage of Pompey's mistakes and make instant, on-the-spot modifications. That is to say, he showed the essential value of flexibility and adaptability amidst the unpredictability of battle. Having guessed both halves of Pompey's mind, Caesar clearly had a better grasp of his opponent's intentions than Pompey had of his. Had Pompey's multitude of oriental horsemen been more battle-hardened, in all probability he might have won the day. To make matters worse, they had been deployed packed too close together and after their initial success, therefore, they lost cohesion and quickly degenerated into a stationary mob. Pompey had kept no cavalry in reserve to save the situation.

Pompey had placed his confidence in the material effect; Caesar had placed his in the moral effect. This is the same distinction that Napoleon drew between what he pertinently calls the terrestrial and the divine. The divine part, said he, embraces all that stems from moral forces of the character and talents, from the power to gauge your adversary and grasp the whole scene, and to infuse confidence and spirit into the soldier. The terrestrial part comprises the war gear, entrenchments, orders of battle, and all that consists in the mere combination or use of routine matters: it does not, in itself, win battles.

Italian faïence bowl (1576), decorated with a scene showing the charge of Pompey's eastern cavalry against Caesar's right wing on his open flank at Pharsalus. Though gathered from ten or more kingdoms and nations, the army's numbers alone made it formidable. The cavalry plan seemed like a battle winner, worthy of Alexander himself. Yet unlike Alexander, who always fought like a Homeric hero, Pompey did not lead the charge in person. (Ancient Art & Architecture)

It was here that Caesar showed his military genius. It was a genius, in the ultimate analysis, that Pompey lacked. Pompey's star had gone into eclipse, though we should resist any temptation to believe that he was beaten from the outset. For instance, his surprise nocturnal attack by sea against an unfinished sector at the southern end of the Caesarian siege lines at Dyrrhachium showed a touch of brilliance (see map on p. 52). With mounting casualties and defeat staring him in the face, Caesar, who could recognize disaster when he saw it, very sensibly broke off the action and marched off into Greece and uncertainty. What now confronted Caesar was the spectre of total disaster, for having run away from Pompey, he was soon to run out of supplies and time.

Unpaid soldiers could fight, but unfed ones would not. Nothing demoralizes an army more than the knowledge that its communications and supply lines, and most importantly its line of retreat, have been cut off.

Nemesis' fool: Pompey at Pharsalus

At Pharsalus, when the two protagonists finally come face to face, Pompey was a weary, worn-out man carrying the burden of his brilliant reputation towards an inevitable end. Pompey, as readers of Caesar will remember, is thought to have despised his adversary too much (an unpardonable crime for military commanders), and been too dilatory in his actions (which seemed cowardly to Caesar). Pompey had his troubles (including a gaggle of senators who pestered him for victory) and his faults (he was overconfident – in a military as well as a prejudicial sense), and it is doubtful too that he was the same man as he had been at Brundisium 17 months earlier. Common experience tells us that the things people tend to overlook are those they learned earliest and believe they know best. For months the two warlords had fought each other, their contest becoming more and more a personal battle, as it had been between Cyrus and Artaxerxes at the field of Cunaxa. At Pharsalus, Caesar was to give Pompey an expensive lesson in tactics.

The legions that made up Caesar's army were trained, disciplined and experienced, and they were made up of men who had fought and bled together side by side, in stark contrast to the situation of many legionaries in Pompey's army. The overall picture is certainly not one of an army of well-trained, military-minded and battle-hardened veterans. Take, for instance, the Pompeian legions from the east, which were composed mainly of the equivalent of garrison soldiers, who were more comfortable with pavement under their feet than the earth of the battlefield. Hence at Pharsalus the Caesarians possessed a moral advantage over their adversaries. Pompey knew that facing facts was preferable to facing defeat. Having little confidence in the majority of his legionaries, he was to order the cohorts to deploy ten deep and await the enemy charge at the halt, hoping to keep his raw recruits in a dense formation and prevent them from running away (Frontinus *Strategemata* 2.3.22).

In this scene we see a much older Pompey, having just ordered his three battle lines to stand fast, witness his front-line men attempting to parry a shower of Caesarian *pila* with their *scuta*. While some of the missiles clatter noisily against shields and bounce harmlessly away, others find their mark. Before long, their retreat would show every sign of degenerating into a rout.

A general view of the port at Brindisi, looking towards the Castello Svevo. Brundisium, as it was then called, was a bittersweet place for Pompey. It was here, sometime in 83 BC, that a carefree Pompey joined Sulla with his private army. It was here, on 17 March 48 BC, that a careworn Pompey abandoned Italy to Caesar, carrying with him several demoralized legions and a gaggle of senators. Thus began the short and tragic history of Pompey's endgame. (Fototeca ENIT)

Cardinal Richelieu wrote in his deservedly much-quoted memoirs that history had witnessed more armies succumb to want and disorder brought about by ineffective logistics than those that faced defeat at the hands of the enemy (1947: 480). This is a matter of 'teeth versus tail', and there is a popular military maxim that amateurs talk about strategy and professionals discuss logistics. And this was Pompey's rationality too, for in the words of Plutarch 'he was determined to avoid battle and planned instead to follow closely in Caesar's tracks, cutting his lines of communication and weakening him by depriving him of supplies' (*Pomp.* 67.1). It was not to be, however, for Pompey was under tremendous pressure from self-serving senators in his camp to meet Caesar in battle and finish the matter once and for all. Hectored, criticized and insulted, according to Plutarch, the great man finally gave way 'and abandoned his own best-laid plans' (*Pomp.* 67.4). By early August the two warlords were to be camped opposite each other on the central plain of Thessaly just north of Pharsalus.

Meantime, back at the empty siege lines of Dyrrhachium, the soon-to-be-defeated Pompey was hailed as *imperator* by his victorious troops, or so claims Caesar (*BC* 3.71.4). The coming victory required that the enemy should be followed with energy. Such was the habit of Caesar himself. It seems that victory is a poor companion, let alone advisor, for in no sphere of human endeavour does Murphy's Law hold truer than in war. Clausewitz called this nasty reality 'friction' – the conspiring of unforeseen circumstances to wreck one's carefully prepared battle plans. Only those who could adapt to circumstances would win. Pompey's campaign, for all its successes, was felt to be doomed, and Pompey himself increasingly looked like a man marked down for divine retribution. As war in its ideal form is nothing other than a continuous series of actions and reactions, the side that develops the greater energy will, all other conditions being equal, become master of the situation. It was Caesar who was destined to harness the physics of military action and reaction.

Death, the final portal

Anyone who has been under a continual strain in action and especially in command knows the weariness that can tempt a man to neglect precautions, take the shortcut, or let things go for once. It is a mood in which the death that may result seems for the moment almost preferable to the unending bodily fatigue and mental strain. The ex-prince of Rome, Pompey, whose fall had been so swift as to be hardly believable, headed for Egypt, where he would be safe once surrounded by those who, as he believed, were supporters of his own cause. As he stepped ashore as suppliant of the Egyptian pharaoh, Lucius Septimius, a member of his personal guard, stabbed him from behind, and with that the might of Pompey was undone. His head was then cut off, taken to Ptolemaios XIII,

A 19th-century engraving depicting the assassination of Pompey as he stepped onto the shore of Egypt. Stabbed in the back by one of his former centurions, he was then ignominiously decapitated by an Egyptian eunuch and his head taken to the boy-king, Ptolemaios XIII. Meanwhile, his naked and mutilated body was left unburied on the beach. In this sordid manner the great Pompey, on the very day of his 59th birthday, passed for ever from the turbulent stage of the late Republic. (Ancient Art & Architecture)

Battle of the Lesnikia, 9 July 48 BC: Pompey vs. Caesar

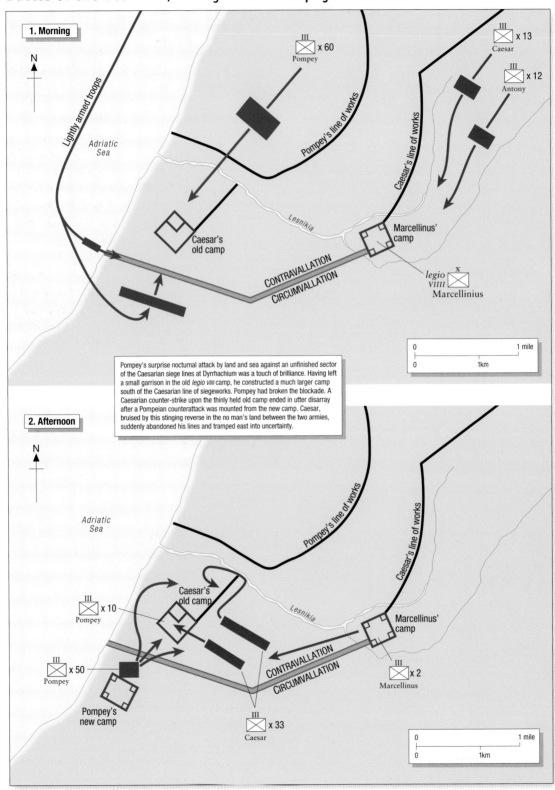

1. Morning

N

III x 60
Pompey

III x 13
Caesar

III x 12
Antony

Adriatic Sea

Lightly armed troops

Pompey's line of works

Caesar's line of works

Lesnikia

Caesar's old camp

Marcellinus' camp

CONTRAVALLATION
CIRCUMVALLATION

legio VIIII X
Marcellinius

0   1 mile
0   1km

Pompey's surprise nocturnal attack by land and sea against an unfinished sector of the Caesarian siege lines at Dyrrhachium was a touch of brilliance. Having left a small garrison in the old *legio VIIII* camp, he constructed a much larger camp south of the Caesarian line of siegeworks. Pompey had broken the blockade. A Caesarian counter-strike upon the thinly held old camp ended in utter disarray after a Pompeian counterattack was mounted from the new camp. Caesar, bruised by this stinging reverse in the no man's land between the two armies, suddenly abandoned his lines and tramped east into uncertainty.

2. Afternoon

N

Adriatic Sea

Pompey's line of works

Caesar's line of works

Lesnikia

III x 10
Pompey

Caesar's old camp

Marcellinus' camp

III x 50
Pompey

CONTRAVALLATION
CIRCUMVALLATION

III x 2
Marcellinus

Pompey's new camp

III x 33
Caesar

0   1 mile
0   1km

Tropaeum Pompeii, col de Panissars (568m), Pyrénées-Orientales, erected by Pompey in 71 BC to commemorate his recent victories in Iberia. Now gone – all we see here are the foundations upon which sit the walls of a late medieval abbey – the monument itself was still visible as a ruin in the early medieval period. Pompey had an outsized personality and a talent for projecting it. Appearances matter, and Pompey's most audacious and ingenious publicist was himself. (Maximillian Dornseif)

and later presented to Caesar upon his arrival in Egypt, while his naked body was left unburied on the beach, the sand tinged here and there with blood. It was to receive a makeshift funeral at the hands of Pompey's loyal freedman Philippos, the ashes eventually reaching the ill-starred Cornelia, to be buried on his Alban estate (Val. Max. 1.8.9, Plut. *Pomp.* 80.6, Dio 42.5.7).

The Augustan poet Virgil, after describing the demise of the sceptre-wielding Priam, dwells upon the contrast between the old king's squalid and miserable end and the glories of his former state, 'he who had once been proud ruler over so many lands and peoples of Asia'. Then he continues: 'his mighty trunk lay upon the shore, the head hacked from the shoulders, a corpse without a name' (*Aeneid* 2.555–57 West). This passage echoes the end of Pompey, once the greatest Roman of his day, scourge of the Mediterranean, conqueror of Asia, and the leading opponent of Caesar, treacherously murdered as a fugitive after his defeat at Pharsalus. Pompey's fame proved no protection, and he died as he had lived: violently.

With their 'Roman' noses and 'Latin' tongue, the Vlachs of Greece (*Vláchoi*) claim they are the descendants of Pompeian legionaries. After their defeat at Pharsalus, so local Vlach legend has it, some Pompeians escaped to the nearby Píndhos Mountains, seen here looking west across the Penios valley from Meteora. (Fields-Carré Collection)

INSIDE THE MIND

Marble bust of Octavianus (Toulouse, musée Saint Raymond, inv. 30007). Octavianus (as Augustus) would be a cure for the poison of the civil wars. (Fields-Carré Collection)

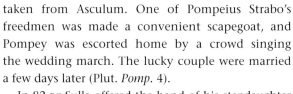

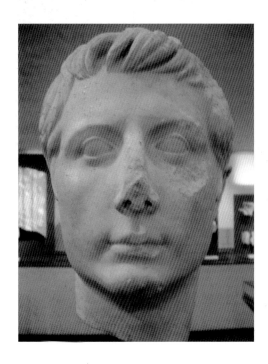

Pompey's multiple marriages are perhaps the least-known part of his story today. Yet his ability to do the right thing at the right moment in most aspects of life, which includes his knack of entering the right marriage, was nothing short of brilliant. His first marriage provides a telling example. His betrothal to the president of the court's daughter, Antistia, secured a rapid acquittal during the trial for the misappropriation of the plunder taken from Asculum. One of Pompeius Strabo's freedmen was made a convenient scapegoat, and Pompey was escorted home by a crowd singing the wedding march. The lucky couple were married a few days later (Plut. *Pomp.* 4).

In 82 BC Sulla offered the hand of his stepdaughter Aemilia Scaura, child of his wife Metella and her previous husband Marcus Aemilius Scaurus (*cos.* 115 BC). The patrician Aemilia – already married and pregnant – abruptly divorced her husband, a man who had dared to criticize the dictator's conduct, and Pompey followed suit by divorcing Antistia. This was unlike the young Caesar, who had refused to give up his wife, Cornelia Cinna minor, in similar circumstances. Besides, it must have been especially harsh for Antistia, whose father had been cruelly murdered by the Marians because of his connection to Pompey and whose mother had taken her own life as a tragic consequence. The new marriage proved to be tragically pointless, for Aemilia died in childbirth soon after. Nonetheless, the marriage confirmed Pompey's loyalty to the new regime and greatly boosted his political career (Plut. *Pomp.* 9).

Pompey's third wife was the befittingly named Mucia Tertia, the third daughter of the *pontifex maximus* Quintus Mucius Scaevola (*cos.* 95 BC), who was to be butchered at the instigation of her first husband. He had been the ill-starred Caius Marius minor (*cos.* 82 BC), and his death at the hands of Sulla had left her as a pawn of the victors. Sulla married her off to Pompey in 79 BC. This marriage resulted in three children: Cnaeus Pompeius Magnus minor (75–45 BC), Pompeia Magna (80/75–before 35 BC) and Sextus Pompeius Magnus Pius (67–35 BC). She had the misfortune to outlive all three of her young. On his final return to Rome, in 61 BC, Pompey sent Mucia a letter of divorce. Cicero recorded the event for posterity, and according to him (*Att.* 1.12.3) the motive was flagrant infidelity – it was even rumoured (Suet. *DI* 50.1) that she was one of Caesar's many affairs. She was living at the time of Actium, and Octavianus treated her with great respect (Dio 51.2.5).

Marble bust of Juba (Paris, musée du Louvre, inv. Ma 1885) from Caesarea (Chercell, Algeria), dated from around 60 BC. The son of Hiempsal and king of Numidia and Gaetulia since before 50 BC, he supported Pompey in the latter's war against Caesar. In 46 BC, after the Pompeian defeat at Thapsus, he was to commit suicide, and his kingdom become a Roman province. His son would marry Cleopatra Selene, daughter of Mark Antony and Cleopatra. (Fields-Carré Collection)

Caesar's consulship of 59 BC brought Pompey a new wife, his fourth. She was Iulia, the beloved daughter of Caesar by his first wife, Cornelia, and his only child in marriage. The autumnal Pompey was said to have been besotted by his charming young wife. Even though policy prompted her union, and she was 23 years younger than her world-conquering husband, she possessed in Pompey a devoted husband, to whom she was, in return, devotedly attached (Plut. *Pomp.* 48.6). Indeed, so much so that in 55 BC his blood-soaked garments caused the pregnant Iulia to be so alarmed that she suffered a miscarriage (Val. Max. 4.6.4, Plut. *Pomp.* 53.3).

The following year Iulia died in childbirth, and her infant – a son, according to some (Vell. 2.47.2, Suet. *DI* 26.1), but a daughter according to others (Plut. *Pomp.* 53.4, Dio 39.64) – survived her by only a few days (Dio 40.44.3). Pompey and Caesar shared their grief and condolences, but Iulia's death broke their family bond, and their friendship began to slacken. Caesar sought a second matrimonial alliance with Pompey, offering his grandniece Octavia, the half-sister of the future Augustus. This time Pompey declined. There was a certain tenseness about the two of them, like partners who might at any moment become adversaries. In time, this rivalry, no longer political but military, would turn from expressions of wrath to those of war.

In 52 BC, Pompey married Cornelia Metella, the very young widow of Crassus' son Publius (killed in Parthia) and daughter of Quintus Caecilius Metellus Pius Scipio Nasica (*cos.*

Marble bust of Sextus Pompeius Magnus Pius, the youngest son of Pompey. After witnessing the treacherous killing of his father, Sextus joined the resistance against Caesar, first in Africa and then Iberia. Surviving Munda, he escaped to Sicily, where he established for the Pompeian cause a strong navy. One of Rome's famous unknowns, he was quickly branded a buccaneer, a desperado, and even an anarchist by the Augustan propaganda circus. (Ancient Art & Architecture)

52 BC), vaunting a matchless pedigree and one of Caesar's staunches foes. Cornelia was a beautiful woman of good character, well read and skilled with the lyre. She was also, says Plutarch (*Pomp.* 55.1), extremely well educated in geometry and philosophy.

Outside the matrimonial bedroom, we know that Pompey had a number of mistresses, and no doubt his fine features helped him greatly in this direction. One particular conquest was the celebrated courtesan Flora, whose beauty was such that she was used as a model for a portrait, which Metellus Pius had placed in the temple of Castor and Pollux. This is the same beauty celebrated by the Epicurean Philodemos of Gadara (*Anthologia Palatina* 5.132.7). Plutarch, our chief authority here, tells us that Flora, in faded dotage, would happily boast that 'she always had the marks of his bites on her when she went away after having made love with him' (*Pomp.* 2.2).

It is Plutarch's fine sketch of Pompey that emphazises the 'hair swept back in a kind of wave from the forehead' and the configuration about the eyes that 'gave him a melting look'. The resemblance of our Roman Alexander to the real one, however, was 'more talked about than really apparent' and 'some people soon applied the word "Alexander" to him in mockery' (Plut. *Pomp.* 2.3–4). Indeed, there was something godlike about Pompey. There was also, his enemies said with more than a little truth behind the malice, something of the prig. He was not a conciliatory man, but one who spurned the use of tact and affability. Pompey was both capable and conceited. He had above all the tiresome ability to arouse in his admirers that kind of veneration that implies disapprobation of those less perfect. People probably cried, 'Pompey is difficult'. He was. He was also the vainest man in Rome.

The convoluted story of Roman politics does not belong here, beyond mention of the fact that there was a plebiscite, the *plebiscitum equorum reddendorum* of 129 BC to be exact, which excluded senators (but not their non-senatorial relatives) from the equestrian centuries of the *comitia centuriata* (Cic. *rep.* 4.2), the assembly in centuries at which all adult male Roman citizens with the right to vote did so to declare war or accept peace, elected the senior magistrates (i.e. posts with *imperium*) and tried capital cases. In 70 BC, Pompey, having gained the consulship, was required, by this law, to give up his public horse. Pompey had held a string of extraordinary commands without once holding a single magisterial position, which meant that he had done so while still only a member of the equestrian order, *ordo*

Colossal marble statue of Pompey (Milan, Villa Arconati a Castellazzo di Bollate) originally from Rome. The plinth bears the inscription 'CN[AEUS] POMPEIVS M[AGNUS] IMP[ERATOR]'. As for other full-length heroic statues of Pompey, tradition has it that this was the very statue at the feet of which Caesar was assassinated on the Ides of March 44 BC. Vivid imaginations have spotted splashes of blood on the plinth. (Guido Bertolotti)

equester, the propertied class outside the Senate. However, his election to the consulship now allowed him entry into the Senate. During his consular year the ceremony of discharging those equestrians who had ended their military service was held in the Forum and overseen by the censors, and they were amazed and gratified to find among those awaiting discharge the consul, in full regalia and leading a horse. When asked how many campaigns he had served, and under which commanders, Pompey enumerated his campaigns, adding, in a loud voice, 'and all under myself as *imperator*' (Plut. *Pomp.* 22.5). After this, his cognomen Magnus, which he had assumed since 81 BC, became his accepted appellation.

To date, Pompey had made many enemies. But even they – although the days of his greatest achievements were still ahead – had to agree that

The misnamed Pompey's Pillar stands on the highest point in Alexandria. Though it was erected around AD 299 to honour the remarkable Diocletianus (r. AD 284–305), it reminds us that Pompey ended his lengthy and glorious career in Egypt. The monument itself was thought to mark the site of Pompey's cremation, a task performed by his freedman Philippos, who had faithfully stayed by the dumped body. In the foreground is one of the sphinxes of Horemheb. (Daniel Mayer)

Pompey knew what he was about. Pompey was a classic example of the obscure man with an inordinate regard for position and the trappings of success, and envious of other people's glory. Here was a man on the make; he was fully aware of the value of celebrity and was active in promoting his own image. Pompey was a great showman and self-publicist, and a smooth-operating expansionist. Impulsive and precocious, he had learned a lifelong lesson: the outrageous statement or action was a sure way to draw attention to himself. Shrewd, sceptical and adaptable, Pompey cast aside old rules, or used them as a screen for pursuing his own ends. Focused and resolute, he allowed little to come between him and his ambitions, which he wore like a second skin. He was willing to use whatever tactic or trick would help him achieve his aims: the end justified the means. In a real sense, he was a man who willed himself into existence, who was, like Coriolanus, the 'author of himself' (Shakespeare *Coriolanus* V.iii.36).

A LIFE IN WORDS

The rather dismal end to Pompey's life when death caught him should not blind us to the masterly way in which he exploited the potentialities of his situation beforehand, bursting the bonds of convention to struggle free for the next episode of his career. As we know, Pompey himself remains mute, and the absence of *commentarii* written by him means that our knowledge of him is derived from his chief antagonist Caesar, the biography of the scholarly Plutarch, written long after the event, and the tart comments of his unwarlike contemporary, Cicero. So his military reputation has suffered severely as a result of the damaging portrait of him penned by Caesar, who wrote, amongst other things, that Pompey 'was reluctant to let anyone stand on the same pinnacle of prestige as himself' (*BC* 1.4.6). Yet this ought not to be allowed to obscure the spectacular nature of his political ascent, which was much more spectacular and much more unconstitutional than Caesar's more conventional early career. Pompey in his early years was a supreme realist as well as an egotistical opportunist. With that, by the 60s, he was Rome's top commander.

When Pompey celebrated his triumph, his third, on returning from the east, it was to engulf Rome for two whole days (28–29 September 61 BC). He had defeated 14 nations and taken 900 cities, 800 ships and 1,000 pirate strongholds. His chariot was preceded by the captive families of three conquered kings, along with manacled pirate chiefs. He boasted of having killed or subjected more than 12 million people and of nearly tripling Rome's public revenues. It was noted that his three triumphs commemorated victories on different continents – Africa, Europe and Asia (Vell. 2.40, Plut. *Pomp.* 45.5, Dio 42.5.2). After Pompey, anyone who aspired to be *princeps civitatis*, the chief citizen in the Republic, had to go much more than just win an ordinary triumph; the price of glory had gone sharply up. Yet there was no room, it seemed, for such a man, no legitimate channel for his influence or proper way in which he could exert his power. There were many who remembered that Pompey had begun his career as one of Sulla's most successful lieutenants, and that it was Sulla who had dubbed him Pompey the Great. And Sulla, who had returned from defeating Mithridates to make war on Rome itself, had set a terrible precedent. In 63 BC Rome had awaited the return of its victorious 'Alexander' with palpable fear.

Ny Carlsberg Head of Pompey (Copenhagen, Ny Carlsberg Glypoteck, inv. 733), from Rome and normally dated to the 1st century AD, perhaps a hundred years after Pompey's assassination. Opinions are divided: some believe that this marble portrait, with its trademark quiff, perfectly captures Pompey's aspirations to be the Roman Alexander, a man with his eye on the main chance; others find the piece, with its puffy cheeks and piggy eyes, a ludicrous caricature of the world-conquering hero. (Ancient Art & Architecture)

The Head of Pompey Presented to Caesar (Caen, musée des Beaux-Arts), oil on canvas by Giovanni Antonio Pellegrini (1675–1741). (Bridgeman Art Library)

If there was ever a right time for Pompey to have imitated Sulla and seized ultimate power in Rome, then it was when he set ashore at Brundisium with the military might that would have crushed any resistance offered. But he did nothing of the sort. His behaviour, when he reached Brundisium towards the end of 62 BC, was more conventional, and more overtly conciliatory than it had been on his return from the war in Iberia. Then, even after the crushing of the Spartacan revolt, he had kept his army together until his election and triumph. Now he disbanded his veterans immediately on setting ashore and quietly entered Rome 'unarmed, with no one to escort him save a few intimate friends, for the entire world as though he were returning from a holiday abroad' (Plut. *Pomp*. 43.3). Whereupon the cloud of fear that had hung so heavily over the capital dispersed. Pompey was obviously more confident than he had been in 71 BC. He was now a consular of eight years standing, and his eastern successes and the adulation they had earned him cannot have been without their effect on his already redoubtable conceit.

Though Pompey was to remain the dominant factor in Rome, he was not to remain the only player in town. Yet in later tradition, as Florus charges, 'Pompey could not brook an equal or Caesar a superior' (2.13.14). Only Pompey himself, comments Seneca (*Epistulae* 94.65), thought that he was not great enough, and Caesar dared to resent the fact that one man stood above him, while the Republic could endure the overweening power of two. Velleius makes repeated use of this theme. In his epitaph on Pompey he observes (2.53.4) that he had risen as high as it was possible for a man to rise. Obviously, on that scale, Caesar wanted to rise still higher. Plutarch quotes a single-verse graffito on a wall in Athens, referring it to Pompey: 'Knowing that you are mortal, you are all the more divine' (*Pomp*. 27.3). An extravagant panegyric, possibly, but in the Hellenistic world, these honours were standard fare for benefactors. In Rome, however, they would have seemed dangerously monarchical. But Pompey, unlike Caesar, had no desire to become king of Rome. Arrogant, devious and aloof, but with no autocratic intentions, Pompey fostered no revolutionary ideas. He was happy with the republican system as long the rules could be bent to accommodate his extraordinary eminence.

Those who claimed that Pompey could tolerate no equal had grasped an important truth, and Pompey's intrigues at the end of the 50s BC were designed to ensure, without resort to civil war, that Caesar did not become his equal. Pompey wanted to make himself the arbiter of Caesar's destiny, ready to protect him from his enemies in the Senate, but was not prepared to condone contumacy. But Caesar had decided to no longer accept Pompey's superiority, that just as Pompey was not ready to acknowledge an equal, Caesar was not prepared to tolerate a superior or owe his political survival to Pompey's charity. He would not serve, only command.

What would Pompey do if Caesar wanted to secure the consulship before he had given up his provinces and army? 'What', answered Pompey very gently, 'would I do if my son wanted to take a stick to me?' This reply puts his position in a nutshell. He saw himself as a father, and Caesar as his son. The *optimates* could rest assured that Pompey would act to keep Caesar in his place, subordinate as a son should be to his father, but they were also being warned that a bond still existed between them as close as that between a father and his son. Similarly, Caesar could read in the words a promise that Pompey would not forsake him but would protect him as a man should his son, but only if he accepted that he owed obedience to Pompey as to a father. Anyway, having got that off his chest, Pompey could turn his turbulent and agile mind to other, more pressing matters.

BIBLIOGRAPHY

Anderson, W. S., 1963, *Pompey, his Friends, and the Literature of the First Century BC,* Berkeley/Los Angeles: University of California Press

Ardant du Picq, C., 1903 (trans. Col. J. Greely & Maj. R. Cotton 1920, repr. 1946), *Battle Studies: Ancient and Modern,* Harrisburg: US Army War College

André, L. (ed.), 1947, *Le Testament politique du Cardinal de Richelieu,* Paris: Robert Laffont

Beard, M., 2007, *The Roman Triumph,* Cambridge, MA: Harvard University Press

Beard, M. & Crawford, M. H., 1999 (2nd ed.), *Rome in the Late Republic: Problems and Interpretations,* London: Duckworth

de Blois, L., 1987, *The Roman Army and Politics in the First Century before Christ,* Amsterdam: J. C. Gieben

Brunt, P. A., 1988, *The Fall of the Roman Republic and Related Essays,* Oxford: Clarendon Press

Burns, A., 1966, 'Pompey's strategy and Domitius' last stand at Corfinium', *Historia* 15: 74-95

Fields, N., 2008, *The Roman Army of the Civil Wars, 90–30 BC,* Oxford: Osprey (Battle Orders 34)

——, 2008, *Warlords of Republican Rome: Caesar versus Pompey,* Barnsley: Pen & Sword

——, 2010, *Julius Caesar,* Oxford: Osprey (Command 4)

Goldsworthy, A. K., 1996 (repr. 1998), *The Roman Army at War, 100 BC–AD 200,* Oxford: Clarendon Press

——, 2003 (repr. 2004), *In the Name of Rome: The Men who Won the Roman Empire,* London: Phoenix

Greenhalgh, P. A. L., 1980, *Pompey: The Roman Alexander,* London: Weidenfeld & Nicolson

——, 1981, *Pompey: The Republican Prince,* London: Weidenfeld & Nicolson

Gruen, E. S., 1974, *The Last Generation of the Roman Republic,* Berkeley/Los Angeles: University of California Press

Harmond, J., 1969 (Diss.), *L' armée et le soldat à Rome, de 107 à 50 avant notre ère,* Paris

Holland, T., 2003 (repr. 2004), *Rubicon: The Triumph and Tragedy of the Roman Republic,* London: Abacus

Keegan, J., 1987, *The Mask of Command,* London: Jonathan Cape

Keppie, L. J. F., 1984 (repr. 1998), *The Making of the Roman Army,* London: Routledge

Kromayer, J. & Veith, G., 1928, *Heerwesen und Kriegführung der Griechen und Römer,* München: C. H. Beck

Lacey, W. K., 1978, *Cicero and the End of the Roman Republic,* London: Hodder & Stoughton

Lazenby, J. F., 1959, 'The conference at Luca and the Gallic War: a study in Roman politics, 57– 55 BC', *Latomus* 18: 67–76

Leach, J., 1978 (repr. 1986), *Pompey the Great,* London: Croom Helm

Liddell Hart, B. H., 1991 (2nd rev. ed.), *Strategy,* London: Meridian

Lintott, A. W., 1968 (repr. 1999), *Violence in Republican Rome,* Oxford: Clarendon Press

McGing, B. C., 1986, *The Foreign Policy of Mithridates VI Eupator, King of Pontus,* Leiden: E. J. Brill

Millar, F. G. B, 2002, *The Roman Republic in Political Thought,* Hanover, NE: University Press of New England

Pelling, C. B. R., 1973, 'Pharsalus', *Historia* 22: 249–59

Sabin, P., 2000, 'The face of Roman battle', *Journal of Roman Studies* 90: 1–17

Santosuosso, A., 2001 (repr. 2004), *Storming the Heavens: Soldiers, Emperors and Civilians in the Roman Empire*, London: Pimlico

Seager, R., 2002 (2nd ed.), *Pompey the Great: A Political Biography*, Oxford: Blackwell

Smith, R. D., 1958, *Service in the post-Marian Roman Army*, Manchester: Manchester University Press

de Souza, P., 2002, *Piracy in the Graeco-Roman World*, Cambridge: Cambridge University Press

Spann, P. O., 1987, *Quintus Sertorius and the Legacy of Sulla.* Fayetteville, AK: University of Arkansas Press Stockton, D., 1973, 'The first consulship of Pompey', *Historia* 22: 205–18

Syme, R., 1939, *The Roman Revolution*, Oxford: Clarendon Press

——, 1964 (repr. 2002), *Sallust*, Berkeley/Los Angeles: University of California Press

Tröster, M., 2008, *Themes, Character, and Politics in Plutarch's* Life of Lucullus, *The Construction of a Roman Aristocrat*, Stuttgart: Franz Steiner

——, 2009, 'Roman hegemony and non-state violence: A fresh look at Pompey's campaign against the pirates', *Greece & Rome* 56: 14–33

Yakobson, A., 1999, *Election and Electioneering in Rome: A Study in the Political System of the Late Republic*, Stuttgart: Franz Steiner

GLOSSARY

comitia centuriata	'assembly by centuries' – a popular assembly divided into five property classes, which elected consuls, praetors and military tribunes
gladius	cut-and-thrust sword carried by legionaries
imperator	'commander' – honorific title bestowed on a victorious general in the field by acclamation of his soldiers
imperium pro consulare	proconsular power
imperium pro praetore	propraetorian power
novus homo	'new man' – term applied to a man who became a senator (or consul) from a non-senatorial (or non-consular) background
optimates	'the good men' – those senators who supported the conservative status quo re the powers and privileges of the Senate
pilum	principal throwing weapon of legionaries
pontifex maximus	'chief priest' – Rome's highest priest elected for life
proconsul	consul whose command was prolonged
propraetor	praetor whose command was prolonged
quaestor	annually elected junior magistrate chiefly responsible for fiscal matters
scutum	shield carried by legionaries

INDEX

MORE TITLES IN THE COMMAND SERIES

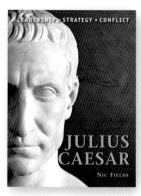

CMD 004 ▪ 978 1 84603 928 7

CMD 011 ▪ 978 1 84908 349 2

CMD 012 ▪ 978 1 84908 317 1

RELATED TITLES FROM OTHER SERIES

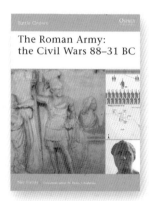

BTO 034 ▪ 978 1 84603 262 2

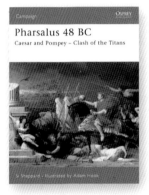

CAM 174 ▪ 978 1 84603 002 4

ELI 155 ▪ 978 1 84603 184 7

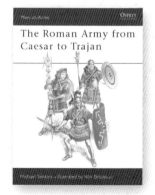

MAA 046 ▪ 978 0 85045 528 1

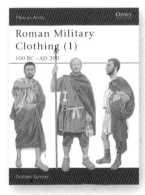

MAA 374 ▪ 978 1 84176 487 0

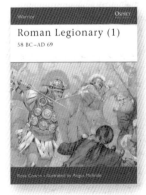

WAR 071 ▪ 978 1 84176 600 3

VISIT THE OSPREY WEBSITE

Osprey Members area ▪ Ebooks ▪ Information on forthcoming books ▪ Author information sample pages
▪ Book extracts and sample pages ▪ Newsletter sign up ▪ Competitions and prizes ▪ Osprey blog

www.ospreypublishing.com

For orders in North America: uscustomerservice@ospreypublishing.com
For orders in the UK & Rest of World: customerservice@ospreypublishing.com

COMMAND

The background, strategies, tactics and battlefield experiences of the greatest commanders of history

POMPEY

CNAEUS POMPEIUS MAGNUS, Pompey the Great, triumphed in a flood of success and blood at 24, and by the age of 35 had reached the heights of Republican Rome and been hailed as the Roman Alexander. His successes against the Marians in the 80s BC, his campaigns in the Iberian Peninsula in the 70s BC, against the pirates in the Mediterranean and his great victories in the east against Mithridates and others pushed Rome's boundaries ever outwards. His military record was second to none in the days of the late republic and was recognized at the time. His place in the historical record has been coloured by his treatment at the hands of Caesar, and this book offers the reader an unbiased treatment of the detail of Pompey's campaigns and his worth as a commander.

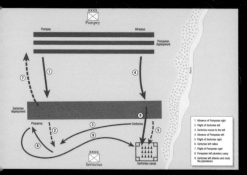

$17.95 US / £9.99 UK / $18.95 CAN

ISBN 978-1-84908-572-4

51795

9 781849 085724

www.ospreypublishing.com

OSPREY
PUBLISHING